MORE THAN
HAPPINESS

MORE THAN HAPPINESS

BUDDHIST AND STOIC
WISDOM FOR A SCEPTICAL AGE

ANTONIA MACARO

ICON

Published in the UK in 2018
by Icon Books Ltd, Omnibus Business Centre,
39–41 North Road, London N7 9DP
email: info@iconbooks.com
www.iconbooks.com

This edition published in the UK in 2019 by Icon Books Ltd

Sold in the UK, Europe and Asia
by Faber & Faber Ltd, Bloomsbury House,
74–77 Great Russell Street,
London WC1B 3DA or their agents

Distributed in the UK, Europe and Asia
by Grantham Book Services,
Trent Road, Grantham NG31 7XQ

Distributed in the USA
by Publishers Group West,
1700 Fourth Street, Berkeley, CA 94710

Distributed in Australia and New Zealand
by Allen & Unwin Pty Ltd,
PO Box 8500, 83 Alexander Street,
Crows Nest, NSW 2065

Distributed in South Africa
by Jonathan Ball, Office B4, The District,
41 Sir Lowry Road, Woodstock 7925

Distributed in India by Penguin Books India,
7th Floor, Infinity Tower – C, DLF Cyber City,
Gurgaon 122002, Haryana

Distributed in Canada by Publishers Group Canada,
76 Stafford Street, Unit 300
Toronto, Ontario M6J 2S1

ISBN: 978-178578-446-0

Typeset in Gentium by Marie Doherty

Printed and bound in Great Britain
by Clays Ltd, Elcograf S.p.A.

CONTENTS

INTRODUCTION

As I was about to finish writing this book, I found myself driving along hedge-lined Devon lanes towards a Buddhist retreat centre, Gaia House. I have been coming here on and off for thirty years or so, attracted by the insights the Buddhist tradition seemed to offer but always questioning, trying to work out whether I could accept the whole belief system or, if not, what I should leave out and why. That journey of discovery had as many twists and turns as my drive, before I felt I could come up with any answers. My relationship with Stoicism followed a similar development.

I am neither a Buddhist nor a Stoic by inclination. The ancient philosopher I feel most in tune with is the more down-to-earth fourth-century Greek thinker Aristotle. But I have come back to Buddhism and Stoicism again and again over the years, despite my difficulties and reservations. Maybe it's because their insights seem to get to the heart of our experience of life in a way that other philosophies don't. I believe both traditions contain much daily wisdom that can help all of us to live better lives.

I know I am not the only one to feel like this. These traditions have proved to be durable sources of inspiration for generation after generation. Buddhist schools that originated anywhere between India and Japan have been thriving and growing in the West since the mid-twentieth century. And Stoicism, which flourished first in ancient Greece and then in

Rome, has experienced a surprising rise in popularity in recent years. After centuries of attracting small numbers of aficionados, there are now numerous books, blogs, online forums and an annual Stoic Week devoted to it. A Stoic approach to business has been advocated in websites and publications like *Business Insider* and *Forbes*. Philosopher Nancy Sherman has explored the relationship of Stoicism to the military in her book *Stoic Warriors*.

Both traditions have helped to give birth, directly or indirectly and with much shedding of detail, to a number of therapeutic techniques that in recent years have swept through the US and the UK, rapidly spreading to other countries. In particular, Stoicism is one of the inspirations behind Cognitive Behaviour Therapy (CBT), while Buddhist meditation is the source of a range of mindfulness-based interventions that aim to help with various conditions such as chronic pain, stress and depression.

Both Buddhism and Stoicism promise no less than unlocking the door to peace of mind and the end of suffering. Yet this comes at a price. Both are radical systems that ask much of their followers: ultimately, to challenge and curb their attachment to the things of the world. Perhaps their appeal lies precisely in this radical nature. More moderate thinkers like Aristotle and Epicurus, a contemporary of the early Stoics, are not enjoying such a resurgence.

I have struggled with aspects of both traditions. It's not only that they are demanding. They are also inevitably interlaced with antiquated ideas, so it is a challenge to extract a message that is at ease in the modern world. We tend nowadays to adopt a naturalistic outlook, one that seeks to explain the universe without reference to anything supernatural. This seems right: our beliefs should be compatible with our best science, which is thoroughly naturalistic. When we are tempted to tolerate aspects of the Buddhist or Stoic traditions that clash with this naturalistic worldview, we risk taking too much from them. On the other hand, we might take too little if we end up borrowing only a few tips in the service of a conventional notion of happiness, so that the radical content is all but lost. In this book I try to walk a tightrope between too much and too little.

My main aim is to explore what we may extricate that fits in with a naturalistic, questioning point of view, but that is more than just tips on how to be happy, as happiness is not everything. This is why I've chosen to concentrate on the parts of both traditions that have the potential to make an impact on how we live, but that also stand up to scrutiny and preserve something of their original radical nature – challenging rather than indulging received notions of who we are and what our aims in life should be.

Both traditions placed great value on seeing things clearly, so rejecting their more outmoded ideas is actually more faithful to their spirit. As Seneca put it, 'Our predecessors achieved a great deal, but their work is still unfinished.'[1] We should feel comfortable putting aside the doctrines that don't quite square up: freezing them in time is no way to pay homage to the creative thinkers who shaped them.

There are many 'Buddhisms' and 'Stoicisms'; therefore the versions I present in this book are composites. I have focused on early Buddhism partly because I find its relative simplicity most congenial, and partly because it seems more readily comparable with Stoicism. And I have quoted mainly from the Roman Stoics partly because of their emphasis on ethical issues, and partly because only fragments remain of the earlier works. I have made liberal use of quotations from ancient sources of both traditions to let the authors' voices speak for themselves.

In light of our profound ignorance of what the Buddha actually said, whenever I write 'the Buddha says' it should be read as 'the Buddha is reported as saying'. I use the Pāli rather than Sanskrit form of words, apart from 'karma' and 'nirvana', which are now terms in common usage.[2]

With huge literatures to deal with, and a short space in which to deal with them, my choice of what to cover has had to be ruthlessly lean, and therefore my presentation is highly selective.[3] I have tried to keep it simple and capture the spirit rather than follow the letter. I am certainly not trying to say anything about what authentic Buddhism or Stoicism should be.

What follows is a personal perspective – which has emerged both from my lifelong search and from engaging with the material – on how to approach these traditions so as to take what we need from them and not more. Along the way, I highlight many of the strategies advocated in both traditions, and in the concluding chapter I describe the ideas and practices that I think we could all benefit from adopting. I hope to show that with the right approach a wealth of inspiration can be ours.

Chapter 1

SETTING THE SCENE

What do we really know?

Bodh Gaya, in the Indian state of Bihar, is nowadays a busy part of the world, full of crowded, noisy temples. Buddhist pilgrims from the four corners come to pay homage to the place where the Buddha is said to have attained his awakening, under a *Ficus religiosa* – subsequently also known as a Bodhi tree. The current tree is just over a century old, although its lineage is supposed to go back to the original tree. We don't really know. The truth is that we don't really know much about the story of the Buddha at all.

The kernel from which the legend of the Buddha grew might go something like this: Gotama, the future Buddha, lived at some point in the fifth century BCE and died sometime around 400 BCE, give or take twenty years. He probably lived at least part of his life in north-eastern India. At that time in India there was an established culture of wanderers and renouncers – people who had given up a conventional social role and become mendicants, dedicating themselves to the spiritual life. What this meant exactly was understood differently by different groups, but it generally revolved around ascetic practices and meditative techniques. Gotama left a comfortable background to pursue this lifestyle, sought instruction from teachers and experimented with but ultimately rejected extreme asceticism. Eventually he had an awakening, a powerful transformative experience that led him to establish a small group of followers at first, and then teach all over northern India for many years, dying in old age.

The texts embellish this story with many details, some more fantastical than others. The future Buddha, for instance, descends from Tusita heaven into his mother's womb. His birth is accompanied by many portents, such as being welcomed by gods and the appearance of a splendid light. The priests declare to his father, a king, that his son has the marks of a Great Man, predicting he will become either a great king or a Buddha. He is brought up in luxury but becomes disillusioned with his life through a series of encounters: with an old man, a sick man, a dead man and an ascetic. This prompts his departure and subsequent spiritual search, enlightenment and teaching.

While its bare bones may well have some historical basis, the story of the Buddha is to be taken as legend rather than biography. A similar story was also told of a disciple of the Buddha, Vasa: 'The son of a wealthy gildmaster in Vārānasi, he wakes up one night with feelings of disgust for the life of licentious luxury that surrounds him. He escapes from the house and the city gates open miraculously for him. However, instead of having to search for a religious teacher, he goes straight to Śākyamuni who is teaching in the Deer Park.'[1] Was this a common story of the time, maybe some kind of ideal life trajectory?

More than that, the story of the Buddha's life as it is usually told also applies to all the other Buddhas that are said to have preceded Gotama, of which there are a few. In one discourse the Buddha tells the story of his manifold previous lives, starting with Buddha Vipassī 91 aeons ago (an aeon being basically a very long period of time), through to the Buddhas Sikhī, Vessabhū, Kakusandha, Konāgamana and Kassapa, and ending with the current Buddha. Similarities and differences are listed: which clan they belonged to, under what tree they were awakened and so on. Lifespan, through these countless aeons, reduced from 80,000 years in the time of Vipassī, to scarcely a hundred in the time of Gotama.[2]

Differences in timescale and detail notwithstanding, the essentials are the same. Vipassī's biography has exactly the same turning points as Gotama's: the descent from Tusita heaven; the encounters with an old man, a sick man and a dead man; the decision to leave his comfortable surroundings to embrace the homeless spiritual life; the awakening; the teaching. This generic Buddha-story may well have preceded the full telling of Gotama's life in the Buddhist texts, which seems to suggest that the life course described is more like a typical Buddha's CV than a historical record.

The appeal of the idea that there is history and biography lurking in the early Buddhist texts if only we can discover it is irresistible, but it has been discarded as wishful thinking by more than one scholar. The story of the Buddha was never intended as pure history. These texts are the stuff of myth and legend and so they will remain. There may well have been a real person at the root of the Buddha's legend, but history and myth cannot be disentangled.[3]

As for the Buddha's teachings, despite modern books having titles like *What the Buddha Taught*, we don't really know what that was either. The main body of work that has been handed down over the centuries as containing the teachings of the Buddha is known as the Pāli Canon. This is divided into three areas: discourses (*suttas*), monastic rules and commentaries.

The texts that make up the Pāli Canon had been transmitted orally for centuries before being committed to writing. It seems that individual followers would specialise in reciting particular kinds of texts, and there would be scope for adjusting length, or detail, according to context. The Canon manifests all the features of oral literature: mnemonic formulae, overlapping lists, repetitions, stock descriptions (sometimes ending up in the wrong places). The doctrinal discrepancies and contradictions that show up in the texts could be due to several reasons, for instance that teachings varied according to context and purpose, that competing schools left their mark in different places, or that doctrines from non-Buddhist schools were gradually incorporated.

Contemporary scholarship is split between those who believe it is possible somehow to isolate the original teachings from later interpretations and those who are more sceptical. But even if we believe that at least some of those teachings have been preserved in the Canon, it would be naive to think that this records the words of the Buddha exactly as he spoke them. Even the early discourses would have undergone potentially major changes in the few generations after the Buddha, and probably reflect later developments. Late additions are likely to be found cheek by jowl with earlier material. The layers are likely to be so interwoven as to make it extremely challenging, maybe impossible, to separate the Buddha's own thought from that of those who followed him.

We know a little more about Stoicism. The school was founded by Zeno of Citium around 300 BCE. Its name came from the location of Stoics' meetings: the *Stoa Poikile*, or painted porch, in Athens' city centre. This is now an unkempt, fenced-off area where cats roam and adjacent buildings are adorned with graffiti. But at the time it was part of a busy public area, where many other philosophical schools were peddling their wares: Cynics and Epicureans were active, and older centres of learning like Plato's Academy and Aristotle's Lyceum were still open. Zeno was followed by Cleanthes and then Chrysippus as head of the Stoics, the latter often considered the most significant early Stoic figure. Teaching continued until sometime in the first century BCE, when the centre of gravity of the tradition shifted to Rome, by then the main cultural centre of the Western world.

But a lot is unknown. The writings of the early, Greek Stoic philosophers are mostly lost, their ideas known mainly through other writers' accounts. This is why reconstructing their views is an uncertain task, especially since those later authors were often hostile towards Stoicism. The work of the Roman Stoics – Epictetus, Seneca, Marcus Aurelius – on the other hand, has survived through the centuries, either as writings by the philosophers themselves or as notes taken by their students. By the beginning of the third century CE the Stoic school was declining, but the Roman Stoics continued to influence philosophers and psychologists with almost unbroken popularity until today.

Similarities between Hellenistic philosophical schools (dating from the fourth century BCE, the time of Alexander the Great) and early Indian philosophy are often remarked on. There are intriguing, if wispy, glimpses of cultural transmission between India and the Greek world, but few hard facts. The geographical link between the two cultural spheres was the vast area covered first by the Persian Empire and then by the empire of Alexander the Great, through which trade and diplomatic routes developed. The Buddhist scholar Stephen Batchelor remarks that there was no 'East' and 'West' at that time, and that the 'world of the 5th and 4th centuries BCE that extended from Athens to Pāṭaliputta was in many respects a single, interactive cultural sphere.'[4]

A central character in this story is the Greek sceptical philosopher Pyrrho of Elis, who around 334 BCE travelled to north-east India with Alexander the Great. He wrote nothing himself, but we know something of his thought through other authors' texts. Diogenes Laertius, who documented the lives of Greek philosophers, tells us that meeting Indian sages led Pyrrho 'to adopt a most noble philosophy ... taking the form of agnosticism and suspension of judgement', and that this was held to bring with it 'tranquillity like its shadow'.[5] One recent, controversial, theory holds that Pyrrho's ideas advocating letting go of all views actually derive from Buddhism.[6]

Diogenes also tells us that Pyrrho 'led a life consistent with this doctrine, going out of his way for nothing, taking no precaution, but facing all risks as they came, whether carts, precipices, dogs or what not'.[7] On the other hand we are also told that Pyrrho lived to be nearly 90, so perhaps we should take these reports of carelessness with a pinch of salt.

Another noteworthy character is the Greek ambassador Megasthenes, who travelled in India around 305 BCE. Again, his writings have not survived, although some of what he wrote was preserved by other authors. Apparently Megasthenes mentioned two kinds of sects: the '*Brachmanes*' and the '*Sarmanes*' – the latter divided into forest-dwellers, living on fruits and leaves, and 'physicians', who lived in towns. These terms seem to correspond to the more common distinction between *brāhmaṇa and samaṇa*. *Brāhmaṇa*, or brahmins, were members of a priestly class dedicated to maintaining the religious tradition rooted in the ancient Indian texts called the Vedas. *Samaṇa* were wandering ascetics, whose movement the Buddha is said to have initially joined.

We can't be sure whether there was any direct philosophical influence of India on Greece or Greece on India, and if so what exactly it was, but this remains a fascinating issue that underscores the striking parallels between Buddhism and Stoicism.

Are Buddhism and Stoicism religions?

Some belief systems form complete wholes and require followers to sign up to every tenet, making it harder to borrow ideas from them. This is especially true of religions. Buddhism is usually classified as a religion, although this is often disputed. Stoicism on the other hand is normally considered a philosophy, although it has some features in common with religions. Neither fits neatly into our current template of what a religion is. But then it all depends on what we mean by 'religion'.

Defining religion is hard: there is probably no one

definition that captures everything that at one time or other has been considered religious, and if we're not careful we can end up with one so broad that it catches all sorts of non-religious stuff into its net. For example, according to the psychologist William James:

> 'the life of religion ... consists of the belief that there is an unseen order, and that our supreme good lies in harmoniously adjusting ourselves thereto.'[8]

James' definition errs on the side of inclusivity. If we were to adopt it, then both Buddhism and Stoicism would qualify as religions. Whether we conceive of religion so liberally or not, this kind of definition draws attention to the fact that the traditions may not best be seen as simple self-help methods, because they rest on complex ideas about the nature and structure of ultimate reality (what is known as *metaphysics*). This might not be obvious from popular books, in which what is more unpalatable is often quietly edited out, as if it were never there.

It's a well-known fact that the Buddha made pronouncements against metaphysics, as his concern was mainly practical. In one discourse the monk Māluṅkyāputta starts brooding on the fact that the Buddha has left certain things unaddressed – things like whether the world is eternal, whether it is infinite, the relationship between body and soul, what happens after death. So he decides to go to the Buddha to sort it out. If the Buddha were to refuse to answer, he would return to ordinary life. The Buddha rebukes the monk, producing the famous simile of the arrow:

'It is as if, Māluṅkyāputta, there were a man struck
by an arrow that was smeared thickly with poison;
his friends and companions, his family and relatives
would summon a doctor to see to the arrow. And the
man might say, "I will not draw out this arrow so long
as I do not know whether the man by whom I was
struck was of the Brahman, Ruler, Trader, or Servant
class" ... or ... "so long as I do not know his name and his
family ... whether he was tall, short or of medium
height ... whether he was black, brown or light-
skinned ... whether he comes from this or that village,
town or city ..."'⁹

He continues in the same tone about what kind of bow or
bow-string it was, what the arrowhead was like and so on.
The Buddha explains that the spiritual life does not involve
settling all questions regarding the ultimate nature of reality,
because this 'is not relevant to the goal', which is nothing less
than ending suffering:

'Whether one holds the view that the world is eternal
or the view that it is not eternal, there is still birth, ageing, death, grief, despair, pain, and unhappiness – and it
is the destruction of these here and now that I declare.'

In another discourse, the Buddha tells the story of a monk
who is curious about where the four elements that make up
the world 'cease without remainder', and who, being able to
access the god-realms in meditation, asks the same question
to ever-ascending hierarchies of gods. They don't know. He

finally appeals to the all-seeing, all-powerful god Brahmā for an answer, but in a strangely humorous twist the great god takes the monk aside and confesses that even he doesn't know the answer.

The Buddha's lack of interest in metaphysics sits alongside a reluctance to foreground supernatural powers or causes. In the same discourse, for instance, the Buddha has to deal with the householder Kevaddha, who is urging him to get 'some monks to perform superhuman feats and miracles' to impress the locals. The Buddha replies that's not his style. When Kevaddha insists, the Buddha goes on to say that while he allows the miracles of psychic power and telepathy, he knows they would be misattributed to charms if displayed, and therefore 'I dislike, reject and despise them.'[10]

But despite the Buddha's reservations, the supernatural pervades the texts. The Buddhist cosmos is thick with gods. The Buddha and his followers lived among and interacted with 'fairies, demons, goblins, ghosts, nymphs, dragons, angels, as well as various gods'.[11]

And while the Buddha clearly disliked showy displays, a number of discourses set out the supernatural abilities that can be achieved through meditative states. In addition to powers like mind reading and recollection of past lives, the ascetic life yields the following fruits:

'being one, [the monk] becomes many, being many he becomes one; he appears then vanishes; he passes unhindered through house walls, through city walls, and through mountains as if through air; he rises up out of the earth and sinks down into it as if it were water; he

> walks on water as if it were solid like earth; he travels
> through the sky cross-legged as if he were a bird with
> wings; he touches and strokes with his hand things of
> such power and energy as the sun and moon; he has
> mastery with his body as far as the world of Brahmā.'[12]

Many people protest that all this supernatural stuff is a late addition to the more minimalist and purer original message. Perhaps because of some of the Buddha's pronouncements, a scholarly tradition developed according to which Buddhism is really a down to earth philosophy onto which supernatural beings and metaphysical flourishes were stuck.[13]

But this may be wishful thinking. A wandering ascetic of the time of the Buddha is likely to have believed many things we find improbable. The supernatural is inextricably woven into the fabric of Buddhism. It is possible to create a 'bespoke' Buddhism by selecting the texts that suit us and leaving contradictory ones out, but that would be moulding Buddhism in our own image. Supernatural and naturalistic aspects of Buddhist doctrine are deeply intertwined. If Buddhism is practical or non-metaphysical, it is so only relatively.

Even away from supernatural beings and extrasensory powers, some key Buddhist ideas are uneasily squared with a naturalistic worldview. Much of the Buddhist edifice is built on the twin foundations of karma and rebirth. It is not entirely clear where these concepts originally came from, but they became common and widespread in ancient India. The basic idea of karma is that our intentional actions (which in Buddhism include purely mental states like intentions and volitions) accumulate and continue to produce consequences well beyond the end of this life, directing us towards a good or bad rebirth.

The idea that Buddhism is a purely secular philosophy devoid of religious or supernatural elements, therefore, is not entirely in tune with its teachings as they have been handed down. The question for the secular-minded is how many Buddhist ideas can survive being uprooted from the religious soil in which they grew.

What of Stoicism's relationship to metaphysics? Like Buddhism, it is far from being a mere collection of wise maxims about how to live and is very much an integrated system in which the practical advice relies on views about the cosmos and our place in it.

According to Diogenes Laertius, for the Stoics God is:

> 'a living being, immortal, rational, perfect or intelligent in happiness, admitting nothing evil, taking providential care of the world and all that therein is, but he is not of human shape. He is, however, the artificer of the universe and, as it were, the father of all'.[14]

The Stoic God can be difficult to pin down. Without going into too much detail at this stage, according to the Stoics the cosmos is providentially ordered by a divine rational principle that suffuses everything. This is what they call God, or Zeus, and sometimes even refer to, in the plural, as 'gods'. Our minds are fragments of this principle, 'literally "offshoots" of God, parts of God that God has assigned to the mind or self of each person'.[15] If this is our essential nature, where does evil come from? The Stoics believed it originates in humanity, but this doesn't seem to get to its ultimate source. It seems that Chrysippus wrote works on fate, providence, divination and oracles, in which he had a go at various answers: cosmically, good and evil are necessarily interdependent; or evil is only a by-product of good; or some apparent evils are actually goods.

Marcus Aurelius was concerned with this problem too. He writes:

> 'Everything derives from it – that universal mind – either as effect or consequence. The lion's jaws, the poisonous substances, and every harmful thing – from thorns to mud ... are by-products of the good and the beautiful.'[16]

It is unclear to what extent the Stoics believed in a traditional person-like God. The Stoic Cleanthes' *Hymn to Zeus* appears to indicate that they did:

> 'Zeus, giver of all, you of the dark clouds, of the
>   blazing thunderbolt,
> save men from their baneful inexperience
> and disperse it, father, far from their souls; grant that
>   they may achieve
> the wisdom with which you confidently guide all with
>   justice
> so that we may requite you with honour for the
>   honour you give us
> praising your works continually, as is fitting for
>   mortals'.[17]

On the other hand, this and other similar verses could be read not as straightforward prayers but as direct addresses to a more rational part of ourselves, like in these lines by Seneca:

> 'You need not raise your hands to heaven; you
> need not beg the temple keeper for privileged access,
> as if a near approach to the cult image would give us a
> better hearing. The god is near you – with you – inside
> you.'[18]

There is a tension between a religious reading of the Stoic God, in which God is the providential architect of the world, and a more naturalistic reading, in which all this God talk is just a traditional way of referring to natural processes. Either way, nature is an expression of a divine rational principle and God is part of nature rather than a supernatural deity standing outside it. Perhaps because this was not religion in the most traditional sense, already in ancient times the sincerity of the Stoics' religious intentions was doubted, and they were accused of bringing in God to give an appearance of piety.[19] Although the Stoics' religious beliefs were relatively pared down, however, they did deeply affect their views on how we should conduct our lives.

The question we need to address is this: to what extent are supernatural and metaphysical elements essential to provide a foundation for ethical and practical advice? Does it really make sense to take only parts of these traditions to help ourselves to live flourishing lives, as is our aim in this book? As philosopher Owen Flanagan asks:

'Imagine Buddhism without rebirth and without a karmic system that guarantees justice ultimately will be served, without nirvana, without bodhisattvas flying on lotus leaves, without Buddha worlds, without nonphysical states of mind, without any deities, without heaven and hell realms, without oracles, and without lamas who are reincarnations of lamas. What would be left?'[20]

What indeed. This is what we'll try to grapple with in this book, about both traditions. In the next two chapters I will look at how they view the *causes* of the human predicament, and in the following two chapters at the *solutions* they offer. Then in the second part of the book I will move on to some reflections and perspectives on what gems may be left if we discard the more metaphysical aspects.

Chapter 2

DUKKHA HAPPENS: WE SUFFER

The human condition

Life is not for the fainthearted. Just listen to the news. There are natural disasters: earthquakes, volcanic eruptions, floods, droughts, tsunamis, epidemics. There are human-caused afflictions: robbery and murder, war, terrorism, discrimination, child abuse, domestic violence, racism, slavery, genocide, environmental destruction and people being generally nasty to each other. Turning to look inside, even the sunniest person is unlikely to dodge forever some version of grief, fear, regret, anger, loneliness.

It's the human condition. Of course, we don't suffer all the time. If we're very lucky, plenty of joy and thrills will come our way alongside the angst and the distress, and suffering will be minimal. If we're very unlucky – our lives blighted by war, poverty, disease – the stream of suffering can outweigh the good. But whether we're lucky or unlucky, death will be waiting. The pain of losing loved ones and the knowledge that at some point we will cease to run around on this earth are things that the fortunate and the unfortunate have to share.

That a lifetime of busyness and striving to improve our life – make it perfect even – should end in death seems absurd, sometimes to the point of draining all meaning out of life. Who could blame us for wanting to forget all about it? And yet the awareness is there, poking us, not letting us avert our gaze for too long.

Many artists and poets have expressed this despair. I remember one of them well from my school days. For Giacomo Leopardi, the deeply pessimistic nineteenth-century Italian poet, human life is like a white-haired, frail, barefoot old man who, carrying a heavy load, traverses mountains and valleys, through sharp rocks and deep sand and thickets, through winds and storms, through heat and frost, through rivers and ponds. He runs, stumbles, gets up, hurries more and more with no rest or sustenance, bleeding and with his clothes torn. He finally gets where all this effort has taken him: a huge frightful ravine, in which he falls, forgetting everything.[1] As a life vision, it doesn't get much bleaker than that.

For a more minimalist version of a similar sentiment, we probably couldn't improve on Nabokov: 'The cradle rocks above an abyss, and common sense tells us that our existence is but a brief crack of light between two eternities of darkness.'[2]

Like other animals, we have a strong inbuilt desire for our life to continue and a fear of it ending. Unlike other animals, who experience fear only when death seems imminent, we can brood on it and stoke the terror well away from any actual threat. Also unlike other animals, we are aware of the ultimate futility of our endeavours.

We deal with this in a number of ways. According to existential psychotherapist Irvin Yalom:

'Death ... itches all the time; it is always with us, scratch-
ing at some inner door, whirring softly, barely audibly,
just under the membrane of consciousness. Hidden and
disguised, leaking out in a variety of symptoms, it is
the wellspring of many of our worries, stresses, and
conflicts'.[3]

But we can't live in constant fear, so we find ways to chase
the terror away: we project ourselves into the future through
our children, we try to become rich and famous, we develop
'compulsive protective rituals' or an unshakeable belief in an
'ultimate rescuer'.

Death anxiety pushes us in one of two directions. In the
normal course of events we assume that satisfying our desires
will fill the void, and we don't let the abyss put us off embracing worldly things with enthusiasm. Sometimes we get what
we want. This approach – distracting ourselves by pursuing
worldly satisfaction – can keep existential discomfort at bay
for some people at least some of the time. But ultimately it
is bound to fail. Our inbuilt dissatisfaction system will make
sure of that, as we get used to and stop noticing the things we
believed would make us happy ever after, then imagine that
satisfaction will come from something else. This is called the
'hedonic treadmill'.

More generally, we adapt to both good and bad changes
in our lives. At one end of the spectrum, grief about bad news
generally subsides with time. Some changes have longer-
lasting effects than others, however, and things like severe
disability are hard to fully bounce back from. Unemployment
and widowhood also tend to leave lasting scars.[4] At the other

end, the thrill of a new relationship or new house also tends to fade. But even if adaptation does not happen and satisfaction lasts for a while, it won't last forever because nothing does. In the long term we are all going to be thwarted, and the search for worldly satisfaction will remain a wild goose chase.

An alternative response to death anxiety advocates overcoming our entrancement with the world of the senses and seeking a different way out, perhaps in an afterlife in which all suffering will cease. All over the world human cultures have come up with paths offering just such a promise. 'Death anxiety is the mother of all religions, which, in one way or another attempt to temper the anguish of our finitude', writes Yalom.[5]

Grappling with our predicament

Buddhism and Stoicism zoom in on the human condition and offer another approach to salvation. Their way of dealing with suffering rests not on the promise of a blissful afterlife but on a deep suspicion of the urge to find fulfilment in worldly goods and activities. It's not by *pursuing* but by *abandoning* our desires that real satisfaction can be found.

There couldn't be a clearer illustration of how the Buddhist path evolved in response to the inescapable realities of life than the legend of the Buddha. After leading a sheltered existence, on a series of outings he has a number of encounters – with an old man, a sick man, a corpse and an ascetic – that prompt his decision to embark on a spiritual journey.

Other passages seem to confirm the idea that Buddhism is at heart a response to suffering. Once, in his old age, the Buddha is warming his back in the last of the sun. His attendant Ānanda massages his limbs, commenting on how the

Buddha's skin is now wrinkled, his back bent forward, his faculties not so sharp anymore. The Buddha agrees: 'When young, one is subject to aging; when healthy, subject to illness; when alive, subject to death.' He then goes on to say, in what seems like a heartfelt outpouring:

> 'I spit on you, old age –
> old age that makes for ugliness.
> The bodily image, so charming, is trampled by old age.
> Even those who live to a hundred
> are headed – all – to an end in death,
> which spares no one,
> which tramples all.'[6]

These existential themes find echoes in other texts, for instance in these verses from the *Dhammapāda*:

> 'Look at this beautified body:
> A mass of sores propped up,
> Full of illness, [the object] of many plans,
> With nothing stable or lasting.'[7]

One word captures the bleak reality of the human condition: *dukkha*. Usually translated as 'suffering', or 'unsatisfactoriness', *dukkha* is the first of the four noble truths, surely the best-known exposition of Buddhist ideas. (The other three are the origin of suffering, the cessation of suffering and the way leading to the cessation of suffering.) The first translation sometimes evokes misunderstanding: if the first noble truth is understood as 'life is suffering', then it can be reasonably objected that life is not only suffering; it also gives us joy and excitement and delight. But that is not the point. The latter and broader translation, more in favour in recent times, has the advantage of pointing to a universal feature of life: whether we are actively suffering or not, no worldly thing or pleasure can give us lasting satisfaction. This is true however we may happen to feel at any given time. Because both translations are partial, *dukkha* is often left untranslated. However it is glossed in English, according to Buddhist studies scholar Richard Gombrich, the first noble truth 'looks more like an exclamation than a proposition': *dukkha!*[8] A kind of proclamation of suffering.

The first noble truth is introduced in what is traditionally held to be the Buddha's first discourse after his awakening, in which a number of key doctrines are presented. Early on in the text the Buddha introduces *dukkha* with these words:

> 'Now this, monks, is the noble truth of suffering: birth is suffering, aging is suffering, illness is suffering, death is suffering; union with what is displeasing is suffering; separation from what is pleasing is suffering; not to get what one wants is suffering'.[9]

This is a brilliantly succinct, yet comprehensive, description of the human condition. We get old, become ill and die. What we love is snatched away from us, and what we don't wish for turns up in our life. Everything else, surely, is detail. Things break, blooms fade, teeth decay, relationships end.

Fundamentally, how life is *dukkha* is described by three closely interconnected qualities, known as the 'hallmarks' of existence. These are:

- *dukkha* itself
- impermanence (*anicca*)
- not-self (*anattā*)

Briefly, impermanence means that all phenomena are constantly arising and passing, while not-self refers primarily to the fact that we lack a permanent, unchanging core.

Understanding impermanence, which is so close to the roots of suffering, is at the very core of Buddhist teaching. At the end of the Buddha's first discourse, one of the monks has an insight that is expressed succinctly as: 'Whatever is subject to origination is all subject to cessation', at which the Buddha proclaims that the monk has understood.[10]

We can train ourselves to become more aware of this by simply paying more attention to the changing nature of all things. When walking along a street, remind yourself that there was a time when none of these buildings stood, and that none will last forever. When you admire a beautiful flower, remember that you are seeing only one moment in the life course of the plant. More awesome still is the experience of looking at a mountainous landscape, knowing that every contour was carved by millennia of ice, rain and wind.

Our faulty views about the self are just as close to the roots of suffering. The Buddha breaks down our experience of self into a comprehensive list of five 'aggregates', or five kinds of physical and mental processes:

- bodily phenomena
- feelings (this refers not to complex emotions but to a basic quality of pleasant, unpleasant and neutral)

- cognitions (labelling or recognising)
- volitional activities (such as tendencies, desires and complex emotions)
- consciousness.

Of each of these the Buddha asks whether it is permanent or transitory. The answer is that all five are outside our control, lack permanence and are subject to suffering; therefore none of them can be a self.[11] It is assumed that a self must be permanent and beyond suffering. But why should that be?

The Buddha may have been responding to a particular religious view, common at the time, in which the self (*ātman*) was considered unchanging and essentially identical to *brahman*, the ultimate reality (not to be confused with the *brāhmaṇa*, the priestly caste), 'the spirit immanent both in the universe and in individual human beings'.[12] In that view the *ātman* was seen as underlying appearances and could be discovered through spiritual practice. Instead, the Buddha instructs us to remain at the level of our perceived experience of the world and avoid speculating about hidden entities.

The Buddha's main point is easily substantiated by reflecting on our own experience, which is indeed that things are impermanent, ever-shifting and *dukkha*. Nothing is solid, everything is changeable and dependent on everything else; therefore lasting satisfaction is beyond our reach. But does that mean we have no self?

There is definitely something we could call the everyday functioning self: the Buddha was not denying that. He merely denied something that may well be better described as 'soul'. Some scholars have remarked that the denial of self in

Buddhism occurs only in specific contexts. The philosophy of not-self is expressed in certain kinds of meditative practices, such as mentally breaking down the body into its constituents in order to facilitate the insight that what we are is really a collection of shifting parts. But while the self is deconstructed in meditation, the monastic rules refer to monks as persons with agency.[13]

In a later text the self was likened to a chariot: there is no essence of chariot, but we find it convenient to use this word to refer to a particular collection of parts – pole, axle, wheels, yoke and so on.[14] This view of the self should not come as a shock to anyone who does not believe in an immortal soul. If we are made up of biological parts, it makes sense that our 'self' is impermanent, conditioned and bound for dispersal when we die. Of course, even if we understand this intellectually, it does not necessarily follow that we experience ourselves that way: we experience ourselves as wholes, not as collections of parts. In the same way, knowing that the table is made up of atoms does not stop us experiencing it as solid.

This is why Buddhism developed particular forms of meditation to focus our attention on the lack of an enduring self. But even without training, we can all try something similar. If you sit somewhere quiet and pay attention to your experience, you will probably notice sensations in parts of your body, thoughts arising in your mind, perhaps images or tunes. What you will not observe is a self separate from these. This opens the door to the realisation that what you call 'you' is no more than the collection of interrelated experiences.

Stoicism also reflects an acute sensitivity to the human condition. Life is short, we have no control over much that happens to us, and death looms for everyone. When death happens, the temporary arrangement of matter that we once were will dissolve and be lost. Far from being unduly pessimistic, this perspective simply recognises certain basic facts about our existence.[15] People need help to grapple with this fleeting, unsatisfactory world, and that is just what Stoic philosophy seeks to provide.

A sense of mortality and time passing are strong themes in Marcus Aurelius' *Meditations*: 'Everything in flux. And you too will alter in the whirl and perish, and the world as well.'[16] Marcus dwells on the transience of things and the vanity of worldly concerns so poignantly that his *Meditations* have sometimes been seen as the expression of a melancholy sensibility. In fact his notes to himself were simply reminders to face the inevitable facts of life in the right spirit.

Conclusion

Dukkha is real and touches all of us. If we're lucky, ordinary kinds of goals – seeking happiness and satisfaction in worldly things – will work for periods of time, but ultimately they are bound to fail. That things are impermanent is an immutable fact of life. Buddhism and Stoicism are right to draw our attention to this situation, make it vivid, urge us to take it seriously and respond appropriately. Exactly what 'responding appropriately' means is open to discussion. For the moment it will be enough to underline the futility of trying to hang on too tightly to things that will pass. But why exactly does our human condition lead to suffering?

Chapter 3

MALADIES OF THE SOUL: WHY WE SUFFER

Reading Stoic and Buddhist literature we might come across phrases like 'a medical science of the mind', 'treating the diseased soul', or the 'existential illness' that the Buddha set out to cure. Both traditions employ medical metaphors to describe the human affliction, which is that we suffer as a result of the kinds of beings we are: deluded and grasping. The false views we hold about ourselves and the world mean that we value and become attached to things that are neither permanent nor valuable. This erroneous attachment is what needs treatment, and both traditions prescribe a therapeutic path for the condition. For now, I will concentrate on the diagnosis.

We're all familiar with medical explanations of physical health conditions. A medical model might involve a disease, a cause, a mechanism of change based on this cause, and a therapeutic procedure. For example, an infection is caused by bacteria; the mechanism of change would involve eliminating or reducing their population and the therapeutic procedure would probably be a course of antibiotics. Picking threads common to both traditions, then, we could say that:

- the *disease* is our normal experience of life, in which we feel emotions and suffer;
- the *cause* is our incessant craving for and attachment to self and worldly things, due to our ignorance of the fundamental features of the world;
- the *mechanism of change* is educating ourselves to see things as they really are and cultivating non-attachment;
- the *therapeutic procedure* is the prescribed path, which in both cases includes cognitive, ethical and experiential aspects.

The Stoic diagnosis

In the Stoic scheme of things, emotions are the main symptom of the disease. There is some disagreement as to whether 'emotion' or 'passion' is the better translation of the Greek *pathos*. On the one hand, 'passion' is said to better reflect the Greek meaning, while the English 'emotion' is broader. On the other hand, the word 'passion' suggests an especially forceful emotion, and it wasn't only the very strong kinds that the Stoics objected to: 'Stoicism as formulated by Chrysippus was opposed to nearly all emotion', writes ancient philosophy scholar Richard Sorabji.[1]

In Stoicism, emotions are problematic because they are inseparable from faulty beliefs about the world: an emotion always entails a judgement.[2] This makes sense: if I'm frightened, I'm implicitly or explicitly judging that something is dangerous. We also know that the judgements involved in emotions can be wrong, leading us to project badness onto something neutral. We may, for instance, be frightened of cockroaches, even though they cannot harm us.

For the Stoics, however, the problem is even worse, since in their framework almost all our judgements about what is good or bad in life are deluded. This is because they believed that the only things that can be good or bad are virtue and vice. 'Virtue' in the context of Greek and Hellenistic philosophy has a slightly idiosyncratic meaning, referring to something like the excellent performance of our distinctively human functions. For the Stoics, this meant primarily our rationality.

From a Stoic point of view, everything other than virtue is, strictly speaking, 'indifferent', which means that although we might justifiably prefer or 'disprefer' something, we should not mistake it for good or bad. Highly counterintuitively, the Stoics held that we are wrong to regard health, life, love, money, comfort, worldly success and achievement as good, and equally wrong to judge poverty, disease and death as bad. It is from this kind of erroneous judgement that emotions arise.

There are four broad kinds of emotion, which are grouped together according to whether they attribute goodness or badness to the present or the future: desire (good in the future); fear (bad in the future); pleasure or delight (good in the present); pain or distress (bad in the present).[3] For example, when we feel joyful about a job offer or a new relationship, we are making the mistake of believing that things outside ourselves can be good; when we're upset that we didn't get the job or were dumped, we're wrongly assuming that external things can be bad.

If the Stoics are right, the great majority of our hopes and plans – in fact almost everything we want and pursue, as well as everything we fear and wish to avoid – are misguided, as they are based on the faulty assumptions that things outside ourselves can be good or bad, that we should act to acquire or avoid them, and that it's appropriate to be happy or distressed depending on whether we gain or lose them. An emotion is a sign that we have allowed ourselves to think of something indifferent as good or bad.

The Stoic reasoning is that since emotions are judgements, we are capable of controlling and altering them, and are ultimately responsible for them. If we genuinely came to endorse the belief that nothing apart from virtue is good or bad, ordinary kinds of emotion (that don't relate to virtue or vice) should just vanish, and this is the outcome we should seek. (The Stoics did allow a handful of 'good emotions', although these are not emotions as we'd normally understand them. I will discuss these in Chapter 8.)

Why would the Stoics take such a seemingly counter-intuitive position? One answer is that they viewed emotions as unnatural. We might object that nothing is more natural. But for the Stoics, 'natural' and 'unnatural' had very specific meanings. 'Natural' meant living according to reason, because as human beings we partake of the divine rational order and our nature is essentially rational. Emotions get in the way of the functioning of the rational soul, as reflected in Zeno's definition of emotion as 'a movement of mind contrary to nature and turned away from right reason.'[4]

Aristotle, an immediate predecessor of the Stoics, held the more intuitive position that emotions are natural and can be useful, advocating that we should aim to moderate rather than extirpate them:

'For example, fear, confidence, appetite, anger, pity, and in general pleasure and pain can be experienced

too much or too little, and in both ways not well. But
to have them at the right time, about the right things,
towards the right people, for the right end, and in the
right way, is the mean and best; and this is the business
of virtue. Similarly, there is an excess, a deficiency and
a mean in actions.'[5]

According to Aristotle, we go wrong in life because we miss
what he calls 'the mean' – feeling and acting in a way that is
balanced and appropriate to the situation. There is a right
and a wrong way to be angry, for instance. It would be wrong
to display great anger about something trivial, or to direct
our anger at an innocent person. But the appropriate degree
of anger, or other emotion, varies depending on the individual and on the circumstances. It's not easy to train ourselves
to hit the mean in our emotional responses, but it can be
done.

The Stoics disagreed: when it comes to emotions, there
is no such thing as moderation. For a start the pleasant and
unpleasant emotions are too intertwined, and have a habit of
turning into their opposite. Ordinary family love, for instance,
easily turns into hate, as Epictetus tells us:

'Do you not often see little dogs gently playing with
each other, so that you would say, nothing could be
more friendly? But, to learn what this friendship is,
throw a bit of meat between them, and you will see.
Similarly, throw a bit of estate between you and your
son, and you will see that he will quickly wish you
underground, and you him ... Throw in a pretty girl,

and the old fellow and the young one will both fall in love with her'.[6]

We might think that we can manage our emotions, enjoying the good ones while toning down the negative ones, but we'd be deluding ourselves. For the Stoics, it is in the nature of emotions to get out of hand. We can relate to this. In almost every tragedy that has ever been written the catastrophe is due to someone getting carried away by a strong emotion – love, jealousy, desire, anger or resentment.

In support of this slippery slope argument, Chrysippus produced an analogy: when we are walking, we can control the movement of our legs and stop if we want to. But running creates its own momentum, so that it is much more difficult to change speed or stop if we wish to. It is the same with emotions: if we feel anger, or love, for instance, it will be hard for us to stop before we get carried away, due to the emotions themselves taking us beyond what is reasonable and leading us to excess.[7] This is why they have to be struck out. For the Stoics, there is no such thing as an appropriate emotion.

Cicero, who was not a card-carrying Stoic but was very influenced by Stoicism, argues in favour of the Stoic and against the Aristotelian position: 'How could it be right to praise "moderate amounts" of what is evil?' he asks. 'If a thing is bad, it is bad also in a moderate amount.' All emotions 'spring from the roots of error: they should not be pruned or clipped here and there, but yanked out completely'.[8]

For the Stoics, as we've seen, emotions are flawed judgements about the nature of good and evil, and the inclinations and dispositions of the personality that persistently produce these are like diseases of the soul. The good news, from a Stoic point of view, is that there is a cure for these beliefs and judgements, and that is philosophy.

It was Chrysippus, it seems, who got the medical analogy going:

> 'It is not true that there exists an art called medicine, concerned with the diseased body, and no corresponding art concerned with the diseased soul. Nor is it true that the latter is inferior to the former, in its theoretical grasp and therapeutic treatment of individual cases.'[9]

The Roman Stoic Musonius Rufus, who lived in the first century CE, states, 'Just as there is no use in medical study unless it leads to the health of the human body, so there is no use to a philosophical doctrine unless it leads to the virtue of the human soul.'[10]

According to Cicero, unlike medical problems, for which we need to seek a doctor's help, with the diseases of the soul we can become our own doctors.[11] Seneca too writes about helping himself through philosophical reflection:

> 'I am committing to the page some healthful admonitions, like the recipes for useful salves. I have found these effective on my own sores, which, even if not completely healed, have ceased to spread.'[12]

Philosophy's 'medical function is understood as, above all, that of *toning up* the soul', as philosopher Martha Nussbaum puts it.[13] But why would anyone want to accept a doctrine that asks us to 'yank out' all emotions and devalue everything other than moral character? What is to be gained by adopting the philosophical life?

Let us remember that the human condition is not a happy one. The Stoics, like other Hellenistic schools, were motivated by 'the urgency of human suffering'.[14] We can remain stuck in the middle of turbulence and confusion, ignorant of what is truly valuable. Or we can choose the truth and tranquillity of the philosophical path. If we do, we will have to turn our back on what is shifting and vulnerable, stop trying to obtain things that we may lose or fail to get, stop trying to avoid things we can't control, and instead concentrate on seeking only moral good and avoiding only moral evil. The reward is peace of mind and a 'smooth and undisturbed' life.

The Buddhist diagnosis

While the Buddhist tradition doesn't use the language of a diseased soul, it does sometimes compare the Buddha to a great physician, seeing his teachings as the cure for the disease of *dukkha*. The four noble truths each have a medical parallel: the disease is *dukkha*; the cause is ignorance/craving; the desired state of health is nirvana/cessation of *dukkha*; the medicine is the path.[15] Bhikkhu Bodhi writes that: 'The Buddha does not offer us palliatives that leave the underlying maladies untouched beneath the surface; rather, he traces our existential illness down to its most fundamental causes.'[16]

Dukkha is attributed primarily to ignorance in some texts and primarily to craving in others. But in practice both are implicated, as it is ignorance of how things really are (i.e. of the three hallmarks of existence – *dukkha*, impermanence, not-self) that gives our foolish cravings free rein.

There are four distortions of perception, thought or view, which explain where we go wrong:[17]

> 'Sensing no change in the changing,
> Sensing pleasure in suffering,
> Assuming "self" where there's no self,
> Sensing the unlovely as lovely'.

Instead we should:

> 'see change in what is changing,
> Suffering where there's suffering,
> "Non-self" in what is without self,
> ... see the unlovely as such.'[18]

As in Stoicism, the cause of our ailment is that, out of profound ignorance about the way things are, we believe and act on the alluring appearances that present themselves to us, leading us to cling to our 'self' and worldly things. We are fundamentally mistaken in our judgement that by satisfying worldly cravings, happiness and satisfaction will come our way. In a world where all is impermanent and ever-changing, this will never happen.

The message is that by engaging with the Buddhist path we can turn this unfortunate situation around and attain the cessation of *dukkha*. This is a central Buddhist goal: in one discourse the Buddha says that what he teaches is just 'suffering and the cessation of suffering'.[19]

We might think that 'cessation of *dukkha*' simply means the end of all suffering, a kind of state of perma-bliss. But it is a little more complicated than that. The basic fact that we feel pain is not going to change. To illustrate this, the Buddha uses another arrow simile:

> 'Suppose they were to strike a man with a dart, and then strike him immediately afterward with a second dart, so that the man would feel a feeling caused by two darts. So too, when the uninstructed worldling experiences a painful feeling, he feels two feelings – a bodily one and a mental one.'[20]

When an 'uninstructed worldling' experiences pain he cries and wails about it, and at that moment suffers two kinds of pain, physical and mental. Normally when we get an ache we don't just quietly feel it and let it pass. Instead, immediately all sorts of aversive reactions start piling up, increasing the intensity of our suffering: we don't deserve this; we don't need it just now; we're stuck with it forever. After training, however, the pain no longer doubles up. When an 'instructed noble disciple' feels pain, he feels only one kind of pain:

> 'Suppose they were to strike a man with a dart, but they would not strike him immediately afterward with a second dart, so that the man would feel a feeling caused by one dart only. So too, when the instructed noble disciple experiences a painful feeling, he feels one feeling – a bodily one, and not a mental one.'

The reason why the instructed disciple is able to do this is an altered perception of the self. Unlike the uninstructed worldling, the disciple does not cling to the flow of mental and physical processes (the five aggregates), mistaking them for the self, and therefore does not get distressed when what is pleasant changes into what is unpleasant. If experiencing pain, the disciple does not react to it with aversion, but relates to it as just a shifting sensation.

It is said that the Buddha suffered from backache.[21] No one could remove that or any other ache because human bodies are susceptible to pain and there's nothing we can do about it. Similarly, nothing could be done about impermanence, about things changing and passing, about not getting what we want and with tedious regularity getting what we don't want. However, while the Buddha had back ache, he did not *suffer* with it. The lesson is that, with training, we can learn to remove the added layer of distress that so often sneaks in unnoticed.

Compare this with Marcus' view that:

'Either pain affects the body (which is the body's problem) or it affects the soul. But the soul can choose not to be affected, preserving its own serenity, its own tranquillity.'[22]

To achieve this imperturbability we need mindfulness. When Anuruddha, one of the Buddha's disciples, was gravely ill, the monks asked how it was that painful feelings didn't overwhelm his mind. He replied: 'It is, friends, because I dwell with a mind well established in the four establishments of mindfulness that the arisen bodily feelings do not persist obsessing my mind.'[23]

This is a remarkable skill, but one that we can all practice to some degree. When we experience physical or mental pain, the first thing to do is to acknowledge it and allow it to be there simply as a feeling that will pass. A popular and useful acronym to remember is RAIN: Recognise what is happening; Allow the experience to be there; Investigate with kindness; Non-identification. By doing this we can loosen the added layer of suffering and become better able to live with the pain. We will come back to mindfulness in Chapter 9.

But can this extra layer of suffering be removed completely, or can we only hope to reduce it? The same discourse says:

> 'If [the instructed noble disciple] feels a pleasant feeling, he feels it detached. If he feels a painful feeling, he feels it detached. If he feels a neither-painful-nor-pleasant feeling, he feels it detached. This, monks, is called a noble disciple who is detached from birth, aging, and death; who is detached from sorrow, lamentation, pain, dejection, and despair; who is detached from suffering, I say.'[24]

This is the difference between the instructed noble disciple and the uninstructed worldling. Aches and pains will continue, loss and unpleasantness of all kinds will continue, but with training we can come to 'feel them detached'.

Therapies of the soul?
Understanding on its own is not enough. Both traditions rightly saw that in order to overcome habitual illusions we

can't avoid the difficult task of changing established perceptions and habits, and that is why both rely on more practical
methods for effectively internalising the message.

The Buddha prioritised direct, intuitive knowledge
attained through meditative experience over logical reasoning or tradition.[25] Understanding how things are needs to be
complemented by a more experiential insight. Our delusions
about self, permanence and the possibility of worldly happiness are deep and hard to uproot, therefore a large part of the
path is about cultivating forms of meditation that facilitate
that insight.

Similarly, the Stoics understood that, although what needs
to be changed are judgements, some beliefs are so entrenched
that we need more than arguments to shift them. To produce
lasting changes, the arguments have to become embedded in
our being through repetition and vivid practices that affect
us more deeply and forcefully. (I will say more about Buddhist
and Stoic methods in Chapter 9.)

The process of abandoning erroneous beliefs and attachments was seen as therapeutic, and many today emphasise the
link between these ancient ideas and contemporary psychotherapies. It is often said that among the primary inspirations
behind the modern Cognitive Behaviour Therapy (CBT), currently one of the most popular therapies on the market, was
Epictetus' saying: 'People are disturbed not by things, but by
the views they take of things.'[26] And mindfulness-based methods, which can clearly make very positive contributions to
people's lives, originate in Buddhist texts.

But Buddhist and Stoic paths to reduce human suffering
shouldn't be confused with what we now call psychotherapy,

which tends to be much more limited in scope and hands-off about people's values. Both CBT and the growing number of mindfulness-based methods have specific goals – to reduce the impact of depression, for instance, or chronic pain. They necessarily help themselves only to certain parts of the traditions they borrow from – those that suit their particular therapeutic purposes – and place them in a completely different context and set of values. While there are always exceptions and grey areas, asking people to completely rethink their value system is not normally part of the remit of the contemporary psychotherapist. If the ancient philosophies and the modern therapies are both 'therapeutic', it is in a very different sense of the word.

Conclusion

In both Buddhism and Stoicism, then, insight into how things really are can transform our experience. Our problems are caused mainly by wrong views about the world. In Stoicism, the disease is the faulty value judgements that give rise to emotions; in Buddhism, it is the faulty perceptions concealing the fact that everything is impermanent, empty of self and inseparable from suffering. To make progress and be saved we must challenge these views, correct our direction and take the first steps along the path.

We may disagree on matters of detail, but the broad thrust of these ideas is surely right: if we attend more carefully to how the world is, we can become more aware of what is truly valuable and less concerned with what superficially appears to be real and lasting. The source of many of our problems is indeed a mistaken view of what matters.

If 'salvation' is some kind of ideal state of being that contrasts with an erroneous worldly existence, then in one way or another both Buddhism and Stoicism can be considered paths of salvation. But of what exactly does this salvation consist? Both traditions were integrated wholes formed of interlocking, interdependent parts, and in the next two chapters I will attempt to spell out the concepts that underscore their views of salvation.

Chapter 4

HOW TO BE SAVED 1: NIRVANA

There are a number of hotels and spas around the world called Nirvana. There are 'Nirvana' relaxation music CDs, yoga studios, chocolates and cocktails. There is no doubt that in common modern usage this term has become almost a synonym for heaven, at least in the sense of a chilled-out paradise for the senses. But nirvana is no paradise: it's a complex, obscure and multi-layered concept.

Just like *dukkha* encapsulates the Buddhist diagnosis, nirvana sums up the ultimate ideal of early Buddhism. Defining it, however, is more difficult. The Pāli Canon is not a coherent document accurately portraying the views of an individual, but a patchwork of perspectives and techniques accumulated over centuries, with the result that many doctrines are at odds with each other. The Canon we have today partially conceals but still shows traces of internal squabbles and external influences. What the concept of nirvana looked like – if anything – at the time of the Buddha can only be a matter of speculation.[1]

In the texts that have reached us, nirvana refers to different levels of transformation, to be realised either in life or at death.[2] The person who has attained nirvana is called an *arahant*. It seems that the Buddha was not keen to engage in conversation about the exact status of a Buddha or *arahant* after death – about 'whether after death [he] exists, whether after death he does not exist, whether after death he both exists and does not exist, whether after death he neither exists nor does not exist'.[3] Still, the promise of the Buddhist awakening is that in its wake karma will stop accumulating and there will be no more rebirth.

Rebirth was perceived as a Really Bad Thing in the Indian worldview of the time, so escaping it would have been seen as a result worth having. Far from promising a solution to *dukkha*, in this view rebirth only compounds the problem, by stretching our suffering into infinity. It can't be a source of consolation, as it also entails 'redeath'.[4] Permanently exiting *saṃsāra* – the unending round of rebirths – is the only definitive solution to the problem of existence, and this is what Buddhism, like other Indian religious systems, wanted to deliver.

Future rebirths are seen as directed by the laws of karma, which govern our intentional actions, including purely mental ones. Bad karma might be followed by rebirth in a hell, or as a ghost or an animal; good karma might be followed by rebirth as a human or a god. A human rebirth is particularly useful, as it is the one from which we are most likely to exit *saṃsāra*.

We might be tempted to see karma as some kind of principle of universal retribution, along the lines of the saying 'what goes around comes around'. In fact it's nothing but an impersonal causal process, akin to the laws of physics. Intentional actions are like seeds that at some point will naturally produce certain fruits. But karma is dynamic, and how the past shapes the future also depends on what we do in the present: just like an ice cube will behave differently depending on whether it is placed into a cup of tea or in the freezer, the particular consequences of a past action depend partly on the current state of the person who performed it.[5]

Much has been written about how coherent it is to try to reconcile the teachings about karma and rebirth with those about not-self: where exactly is the locus of moral responsibility, who or what exactly is reborn? But we don't really know the relative antiquity of these concepts, and whether the awkwardness may be due to later, ill-fitting introductions.

If, like me, you are troubled by this whole set of concepts and just can't get yourself to entertain the idea of rebirth, it's worth setting it aside for a while and instead exploring the idea of nirvana in life. This is not at all clear, alas, as there are a lot of discrepancies in the way the texts describe nirvana. Is it a blissful state, or even some kind of separate dimension of experience, an 'unconditioned realm' beyond impermanence and *saṃsāra* that the *arahant* can access directly at the time of awakening? Can anything be said about it?

To begin with, nirvana is an experience through which the *arahant* comes to see the world as it really is (i.e. impermanent, *dukkha* and empty of self). This is not the kind of insight that we lesser mortals could have. The Buddha discouraged pursuing a purely intellectual understanding, indicating that this is not the way to awakening.[6] What the *arahant* experiences is a direct recognition of the way things are: a 'seeing as' as well as 'knowing that'.[7] This means coming to see beyond the seeming solidity and separateness of ordinary things and actually *perceiving* the world as impermanent, *dukkha* and empty of self.

Insight and concentration

What practices will most directly get us to that state, it is not easy to say. There are two different meditative paths in the early Buddhist tradition, and their relationship is unclear. Insight meditation (*vipassanā*) aims at this kind of direct perception of things as they really are. Tranquillity meditation (*samatha*) is meant to calm the mind and lead to states of deep concentration known as the absorptions (*jhānas*).

In tranquillity meditation, as the meditator ascends from the first to the fourth *jhāna*, and from there to the further four 'formless attainments', the mind becomes progressively stiller and consciousness narrows, culminating in a contentless state in which all sensation and cognition temporarily cease.[8] This state is unrippled by thoughts or feelings, and external stimuli don't impinge on the consciousness of the meditator. It is a bit like being dead, in that all physical and mental activity has stopped. The texts explain, however, that unlike in death the monk's 'vitality is not exhausted'.[9]

Sometimes this state is identified with nirvana.[10] But while states of absorption may be close to and mistaken for nirvana, they are not the real thing. One difficulty is that nirvana is frequently characterised as necessitating deep insight into the nature of things, and this seems incompatible with such a contentless consciousness. It has been suggested therefore that insight and tranquillity meditations may once have been alternative paths with different goals, the former for overcoming ignorance and the latter for overcoming craving.[11]

Some scholars have seen at least the higher *jhānas*, which involve supernatural powers, as remnants of a separate spiritual strand, characteristic of previous, non-Buddhist forms of meditation. Certain views and methods may have been imported into more specifically Buddhist material from other systems, like early forms of Jainism. These methods include ascetic techniques, such as abstaining from food, and meditative practices that aim at bringing the mind to a complete standstill. Ultimately, the ascetic would achieve complete motionlessness of body and mind and cessation of breathing, whereupon death would follow. This would be a positive outcome in Jainism, according to which karma was the cause of suffering, therefore the aim was to avoid accumulating new karma and destroy old karma through non-activity.[12]

Whatever the historical development actually was, both insight and concentration became part of the Buddhist path, although they coexist uncomfortably, amid discordant notes. There is still a lot of debate about how the two fit in with each other and whether or how much *jhāna* achievement is necessary on the way to nirvana. Some texts seem to suggest that the absorptions are conducive to awakening, even essential for it.[13] On the other hand *jhāna* states are as impermanent and *dukkha* as everything else, therefore they do not ultimately lead to salvation.[14] Elsewhere the possibility is raised that they

may be dispensable.[15] Some texts flexibly suggest that it is possible to approach the two in any order, or pursue both at the
same time.[16]

The *jhāna*s are something of a double-edged sword. Apart
from developing concentration, they perform the useful
function of aiding detachment from worldly delights, as the
pleasure they generate makes those fade by comparison. But
for the same reason an excessive focus on the *jhāna*s could
create attachment – almost an addiction – to those states, so
meditators should be on their guard.

While a number of modern teachers have taken the view
that only insight is necessary for awakening, and that this
can be attained with only a modicum of concentration, the
traditional position is that the way of insight and the way
of concentration are complementary, and the two should be
developed together. You can't develop insight if your mind is
scattered; therefore some concentration is the basis for insight
training.[17]

The relationship between the calm absorption of meditation and insight is captured with a simile: just like we would
not be able to see our reflection in a bowl of water that had
been mixed with a dye, or was bubbling over a fire, or was
muddy or had algae growing in it, in the same way we need a
calm mind to see things clearly.[18]

The basic structure of *vipassanā* (insight) meditation is to
pay attention to the arising and passing of what we experience
in our field of consciousness – sensations, sounds, thoughts,
feelings. In *samatha* (tranquillity) meditation, the starting
point is to focus on an object of attention, which is often the
breath. In both meditations, almost all of us will find ourselves

distracted. When this happens, we simply notice and return to the practice.

Mystical experiences

Insight, perceiving the world as it really is, is the key characteristic of nirvana. But what does that actually mean? Is nirvana a mystical experience? And if so, what kind? There are different ways of characterising a mystical or religious experience. One of the best known is William James', which sets out the following criteria.[19] They must be:

- ineffable (they can't be properly captured in words);
- noetic (they appear to convey some knowledge or insight about the world);
- passive (they arise unbidden);
- transient.

In this understanding, nirvana in this life may or may not qualify as a mystical experience. It is passive in the sense that it cannot be summoned at will. On the other hand, much groundwork is necessary for it to find fertile soil: the insight characteristic of nirvana typically arises after a lot of meditative practice.[20] It is transient, in that the *arahant* subsequently returns to a more ordinary perception of the world. In the standard understanding of nirvana as involving direct insight into how things really are it seems to be noetic: in James' terms, such experiences appear as 'states of insight into depths of truth unplumbed by the discursive intellect'.[21] It is not clear whether it is ineffable, since the perception it embodies may be expressed but not properly captured through language.

The idea of experiencing things as they really are in themselves is certainly alluring. But how deeply can our understanding penetrate? A mystical experience can be so powerful as to create an unshakeable conviction that we have pierced through the surface of things. But, central though such an experience may be in someone's life, could it ever justify drawing conclusions about what things are like in themselves?

The eighteenth-century philosopher Immanuel Kant had a thing or two to say about this subject. He convincingly argued that our experience of the world is mediated by categories such as physical identity, space, time and causal connection, imposed by our particular sense organs and cognitive abilities. Because of the kind of beings we are, we can access the world only through these lenses, and whatever may exist outside our mental and perceptual capacities is forever unknowable to us. 'We can never, even by the strictest examination, get completely behind the secret springs of action.'[22] We should not mistake experience, which is all we can have, for ultimate reality. We simply don't know how accurate our representations of whatever is 'out there' are likely to be.

Like a motorcycle helmet we can't take off, we're forever hampered by human senses and brain: reality is 'veiled'.[23] Although in a mystical experience those Kantian categories are typically altered, it is still a human brain that is doing the experiencing, and as such all it can have is an experience, not a direct apprehension of things in themselves. Much as we might wish otherwise, we have no reason to think that mystical experiences reveal reality as it is.

That does not necessarily mean, however, that such experiences can't help to increase our understanding. Imagine for instance coming to perceive yourself and the world as a web of constantly changing relationships, with no sharp distinctions between self and others. Even if such an experience cannot make absolute reality transparent to us, couldn't it still give us a *more objective* understanding than our ordinary perception of separateness and solidity? After all, we know that behind the apparent solidity of objects atoms are in flux. The question then is what we mean by 'objective'.

The American philosopher Thomas Nagel writes about the uneasy interplay between our own particular subjective perspective and a more objective view of the world. As Nagel sees it, there is no binary division between objective or subjective; it is more like a spectrum on which a viewpoint may be seen as more or less objective. 'A view or form of thought is more objective than another if it relies less on the specifics of the individual's makeup and position in the world, or on the character of the particular type of creature he is', he writes.[24]

We can shuffle a bit in the direction of more objectivity if we move from a narrow understanding of the relationship between the world and ourselves to a wider, more detached one. 'Thus objectivity allows us to transcend our particular viewpoint and develop an expanded consciousness that takes in the world more fully.'

Moving away from egocentric concerns and developing an awareness of the interrelation of all things might move us along the objectivity spectrum. But we mustn't forget, says Nagel, that we belong to the world, and complete objectivity – the 'view from nowhere' – is beyond us: 'Whatever we do, we remain subparts of the world with limited access to the real nature of the rest of it and of ourselves. There is no way of telling how much of reality lies beyond [our] reach'.

As our friend Pyrrho the sceptic philosopher might have advised, it may be wise to suspend judgement about how much reality we can really know. In the end it is up to each of us to decide how much of our life we are willing to devote to the pursuit of experiences that might reveal the true nature of the world to us, when there is no guarantee either of having the experience in the first place or that it would be genuinely revelatory.

Nirvana as an ethical ideal

If we reject ideas of karma, rebirth and direct insight into the nature of things, what is left of nirvana? Some have emphasised its more ethical aspects. It is said that even an evil man may achieve high states of concentration, but nirvana is inescapably bound with living ethically.[25]

Although after nirvana the *arahant* returns to a more normal perception of the world, things are forever changed in light of the cognitive and ethical transformation that has occurred. This results from the fact that the *arahant* has extinguished the three defilements, or 'unwholesome roots': greed, aversion and delusion.

It seems that an ancient Buddhist school, the Sautrāntikas, advocated a deflationary understanding of nirvana as no more than the absence of defilements.[26] The ethical focus of nirvana seems to be avowed in this discourse, in which a wanderer quizzes Sāriputta:

'Friend Sāriputta, it is said, "Nibbāna [Nirvana], Nibbāna." What now is Nibbāna?

> The destruction of lust [greed], the destruction of hatred [aversion], the destruction of delusion: this, friend, is called Nibbāna.'[27]

The Buddhist monk, scholar and teacher Anālayo equates nirvana to 'a condition of complete mental health'.[28] This is a conception of health that goes well beyond our ordinary understanding. According to the World Health Organization, mental health is 'a state of well-being in which every individual realises his or her own potential, can cope with the normal stresses of life, can work productively and fruitfully, and is able to make a contribution to her or his community.' This is already quite demanding, but it's much more limited than anything nirvana might involve.[29]

Mental health of the nirvana kind would be a state of complete freedom from greed, aversion and delusion. This is clearly a far-flung ideal. But even if that remains beyond us, we could aspire to a more down to earth form of it. For instance, a 'little nirvana' could consist in a state of more contentment and less reactivity.[30]

Conclusion

The root of the word 'nirvana' is related to 'blowing out', as if of a lamp or a fire. And apart from the direct apprehension of things in themselves, nirvana is indeed described mostly in terms of what is extinguished. In life, there is the eradication of greed, aversion and delusion, of the karmic fruits that lead to rebirth, and of *dukkha* in the sense of the second arrow that adds mental to physical suffering. After death, there is the end of *dukkha* in the sense of exit from *saṃsāra*.

If we believe that the goals of achieving direct insight into reality or ending the cycle of rebirths are misguided, we inevitably strip away from nirvana much of what it traditionally entails. However, we could retain a minimal understanding of it: the possibility of experiencing pain in a more detached way and the ethical ideal of our actions flowing from non-attachment, kindness and wisdom (the opposites of greed, aversion and delusion). That may not be anyone's idea of paradise, but it's certainly an improvement on the normal conflicted condition of humankind.

Chapter 5

HOW TO BE SAVED 2: LIVING IN ACCORDANCE WITH NATURE

Many of us consider happiness the most important thing in life. People in therapists' consulting rooms around the world say they just want to be happy. And don't parents say that what they want most of all for their children is happiness? At first sight the ancient Greeks appear to endorse this. Even Aristotle says that happiness is the highest good.

In fact, it's a lot more complicated. Aristotle immediately qualifies his statement by saying that being happy means 'living well and acting well'. The fault is really in the translation. The ancient Greeks' word for the highest good in life is *eudaimonia*. This is often translated as 'happiness', but unlike our more usual understanding of 'happy' it does not mean any kind of cheerful mood.[1] It points to something more objective, like having had the kind of life that can legitimately be considered good. More appropriate translations are the good life, or human flourishing. But it was more an abstract ideal than a concrete, specific prescription for how to live.

Eudaimonia always involved some kind of virtue, or moral excellence, but different schools filled in the details differently.[2] For Aristotle, the good life was virtuous activity in accordance with reason, although other things like health and friends and sufficient money needed to be in place for a life to be properly flourishing. For Epicurus, the main ingredient of the good life was pleasure, but this was not – as we might imagine if we were misled by the contemporary meaning of the word 'epicurean' – of the eating, drinking and being merry kind, or any other pleasure of the flesh. Instead, the most pleasant life is one of tranquillity (*ataraxia*), achieved through simplicity and freedom from fear.

The Stoics were at the more radical end of the spectrum. Their ideal was often expressed as 'living in accordance with nature'. You would be forgiven for imagining that a theory that encouraged acting according to nature would advocate letting it all hang out, spontaneously following impulses and emotions. But that would be anachronistic; in fact, nothing could be further from the truth. The Stoic view of nature is unexpected, and we have to dig below the surface to understand it.

A smooth flow of life

As we have seen, the Stoic cosmos was pervaded by a rational principle that they equated with nature, but also with God, with reason and with fate. Our own soul is a fragment of God/ reason, therefore it is in our essential nature to be rational beings.[3] Stoic authors come back to this theme again and again. Musonius Rufus writes: 'Indeed, the human being, alone of the creatures on earth, is the image of the divine and has the same virtues as the divine.'[4] According to Seneca, the human mind 'was not composed of heavy, earthy substance but descended from the lofty, heavenly breath'.[5]

Living in accordance with nature means conforming with the universal principle, which is the same as God/reason/fate. Another formulation of the Stoic goal is 'a smooth flow of life'. This is achieved when we live according to our own nature and the nature of the universe. Other ways of expressing this were 'living consistently' and 'life in accordance with virtue', since virtue just is following nature and reason.[6] It is in this sense that the Stoics considered virtue the highest good. Nothing else was required to have a good life.

We might not recognise these descriptions from our life experience, which is not usually one of unfettered rationality. For the Stoics this is because although our rationality is basically the same as that of the gods, it differs in not being perfect. It needs some tender care, Seneca says:

> 'Seeds of divinity are scattered in human bodies: if a good gardener takes them in hand, the seedlings resemble their source and grow up equal to the parent plant. But poor cultivation, like sterile or boggy soil, kills the plants and produces only a crop of weeds.'[7]

Where does all the irrational stuff come from, you might wonder. The answer is that although we are born free and uncorrupted, with an innate tendency towards fulfilling our rational nature, corruptions creep in as a result of environmental factors.[8] According to Cicero, the 'sparks of understanding' that nature has given us are put out by the 'corrupting influences' through which we acquire 'wrongful habits and beliefs'. This process starts with the family, but it is by contact with society at large that 'we become thoroughly infected with corrupt beliefs and secede from nature absolutely'.[9] However, while these can hinder us, ultimately they cannot stop our drive towards moral development.

In practice, what does it mean to be rational? Mainly separating what really *is* good and bad from what merely *seems* good and bad. Here the Stoics' views are at odds with more ordinary perceptions of good and bad. As we have seen, all the things we are normally attracted to or repulsed by should be of no concern. The main reason why virtue alone is genuinely good is because it is the only reliable thing in life. Nobody can take it away, since it depends only on us. Everything else is fragile, uncertain and liable to slip through our fingers at any point. Also, unlike other things, which can be used well or badly, virtue can be only good, never bad.

Epictetus put this in terms of what is up to us, or in our power, and what is not: we should cultivate the former and disregard the latter. His work is filled with different formulations of this position, but this is a classic statement of it:

> 'In our own power are choice, and all voluntary actions; out of our power, the body and its parts, property, parents, brothers, children, country; and, in short, all our fellow beings. Where, then, shall we place the good? In what shall we define it to consist? In things within our own power.'[10]

He recommends this practice for questioning what is in our power:

'When you go out in the morning, examine whomso-
ever you see, or hear, and answer as if to a question.
What have you seen? A handsome person? Apply the
rule. Is this within or outside your choice? Outside it.
Discard it. What have you seen? Someone mourning the
death of a child. Apply the rule. Death is not within your
choice. Discard it.'[11]

As we have seen, the Stoics had a word for the things that
are not in our power (which is everything apart from virtue): 'indifferents', as they should be exactly that. Diogenes
Laertius left us a handy list of these: 'life, health, pleasure,
beauty, strength, wealth, fair fame and noble birth, and their
opposites, death, disease, pain, ugliness, weakness, poverty,
ignominy, low birth, and the like.'[12]

Epictetus also urges his students to practise denying value
to indifferents:

'[Begin] with the least and frailest things, as with
earthenware, or a cup. Afterwards, proceed to clothes,
a dog, a horse, an estate; then to yourself, your body
and its parts, your children, wife, brothers. Look every-
where around you, and hurl these things away from
you. Correct your views. Allow nothing to cleave to you
that is not your own and may give you pain when it is
torn away.'[13]

We needn't go to the same extremes as Epictetus, hurling
away cherished objects and loved ones. But we could practise
becoming less attached to things that we know on reflection

are not that important. Next time you break a mug, for instance, or spill coffee on a favourite jumper, you could try adopting Epictetus' attitude.

Where Epictetus advised testing the value of things by asking whether they are in our power, Chrysippus recommended the following two questions:

1. Is there good or bad at hand?
2. Is it appropriate to react?

For a Stoic, the answer to the first question would be yes only if it refers to our virtue. Otherwise it would always be no, because nothing external to us is truly good or bad. It follows that the answer to the second question would also be no, it is not appropriate to react.

However, we might find it hard to go along with that. It's difficult to embrace the view that things like health, life and loved ones should all be indifferents, albeit 'preferred' ones. Some might find it impossible to agree that poverty is not an evil. Chrysippus' exercise allows for this, because those who are struggling to let go of 'irrational' ideas about good and bad can concentrate on the second question. Even if their views are still flawed, they can begin to make progress by relinquishing destructive behaviours that are not conducive to virtue. But, for the Stoics, in time we should move on to confronting our incorrect views of good and bad.

Whether or not we agree with the Stoic assessment of what is truly good or bad, surely we do often make the mistake of giving too much importance to things that are of little or no value. To avoid this, we could ask ourselves Chrysippus' questions. First we examine the importance of what we're getting distressed, or excited, or angry about. Sometimes we'll readily come to see that the issue is trivial. But even if we don't, we could do with questioning our reactions, since often we get carried away by negative emotions that lead us to react in unskilful ways. Even if on reflection we conclude that we had reason to be angry, for instance, and that a response is in order, it's best to consider calmly how to deal with the situation.

The Stoics themselves at times softened their more austere position, which seems to leave little room for ordinary human urges and inclinations, by allowing that certain indifferents can be pursued so long as we remember at all times that they are not ultimately good. Then if there is a clash between virtue and an indifferent we will know straight away which to choose. This is Epictetus' colourful analogy:

'Someone scatters figs and nuts. Children scramble and quarrel for them; but not men, for they think them trifles. ... Provinces are being distributed. Let children look to that. Money. Let children look to it. Praetorships, consulships. Let children scramble for them. ... But to me they are mere figs and nuts.'[14]

Praetorships and consulships may no longer concern us, but our modern condition is no different. It is natural for us to prefer to have ordinary human goods such as wealth, relationships, health and life, and equally natural to want to avoid poverty, bereavement and illness. So, while these things fall short of being 'good', they do have a kind of value. If a fig or a nut were to fall into our lap, says Epictetus, let's pick it up and eat it. But if to get it we have to stoop low, upsetting or flattering others, the price is not worth paying.

But normally things don't just fall in our lap: we have to devote precious time and energy to the pursuit of our goals. The question is how much. How hard should we try to improve our health, change our job, or find a partner, before concluding this is not what was meant for us?[15] In some more uncompromising passages, Epictetus seems to reject the suggestion that we can have our cake and eat it, pointing out that we have to choose how we allocate our resources, and that we are liable to incur what we might nowadays call 'opportunity costs' if we put any effort at all into pursuing indifferents:

'You cannot invest your attention both on externals and on your own ruling faculty. If you want the former, leave the latter alone; or you will succeed in neither, as you are drawn in different ways by the two. But if you want the latter, let external things go.'[16]

This suggests that we really do have to choose between virtue or anything external: '"May I not desire health, then?" By no means; nor anything else that depends on another; for what is not in your power either to procure or to preserve when you wish, that belongs to another.'[17]

The Stoic theory of indifferents is subtle to say the least. It is connected with their view that the universe is providentially ordered and arranged in the most rational way, so we should willingly go along with whatever unfolds for us in the world.

But the divine script is not always transparent, and this is why, when we are ignorant of it, we can be allowed to pursue an indifferent. Ultimately, we should give up any goal or desire if it becomes clear that it is not part of the divine plan.

Epictetus likens our position to that of actors in a play. Whatever its divine author wills we do, we should also will: 'this is your business, to act well the given part,' he says, 'but to choose it, belongs to another'. God decides if life is long or short, if we are rich or poor, healthy or sick. 'If it is his will that I should die, or be tortured, then it is also my will.'[18]

If we do seek to obtain an indifferent, we should do so with care, which means 'selecting' and 'deselecting' things in the knowledge that they are not ultimately good or bad.[19] We should pursue things only 'with reservation', or in the full awareness that we might get what we don't want and not get what we do want, just like in the Buddha's definition of suffering.

To sum up, like the Buddha, the Stoics radically redefined the flourishing human life. In the Stoic worldview, the universe is providentially ordered and we are fragments of the divine rational principle that orders it. Virtue is the only good, vice is the only evil; all the other things we love or loathe are indifferent. Virtue and rationality lie in understanding this and acting accordingly. As Epictetus reminds us, this means always remembering that we have no control over external things but complete control over our thoughts and feelings, which we should exercise by investing in choice and character the value we normally allocate to the fragile and unstable items of the world. If we do that, we will succeed in eradicating the emotions and achieving freedom from disturbance. Fully realising this, the sage becomes 'aligned with the real nature of the universe.'[20]

Questioning the smooth flow

There are a number of things we could question in this picture. One is just how much control we have over our inner life. A central piece of the Stoic worldview, which Epictetus in particular forcefully wants to impress on his students, is that while we have no control whatsoever over external events, which are providentially ordered and over which we should lose no sleep, we do have full control over our character and choices. This seems a bit too stark, both more and less optimistic than reality warrants.

It is more optimistic because it overestimates our command of our internal experience. We appear to have a certain amount of control over decisions and choices – more so, it seems, than over external events. It's true that having become aware that we are putting on weight we can decide to go on a diet, or join the gym, and sometimes we actually do it. We can decide to make a cup of tea and follow this up by going into the kitchen and putting the kettle on. It's also true that, having settled on our intentions, we have no say over whether there is a power cut, or the kettle breaks, or some other emergency prevents us from making the tea. When things do go wrong, though, we have some control over how we deal with the new situation.

But the extent to which our cognitions, decisions and intentions are generated unconsciously and influenced by our environment is turning out to be far greater than we, let alone the Stoics, could imagine. As is evident from the work of psychologists such as Daniel Kahneman, while our conscious awareness makes a difference to who we are, it is likely to be only the tip of an enormous iceberg in which most functioning is under the surface and non-conscious. We'll look at this more closely in Chapter 9.

The Stoic view is also less optimistic than warranted because we do have some influence over how external things develop. If we choose to change our diet, or take up exercise, we may be able to positively affect our health, for instance. Having said that, it is of course true, as the Stoics thought, that external events are largely not in our power, and therefore we need to work on accepting what 'fate' brings us.

The much-quoted Serenity Prayer asks for the serenity to accept the things that we can't change, the courage to change those that we can, and the wisdom to know the difference.[21] This last ability is the crucial one, and reason can help us to work out in each situation what to accept and what to try to change.

As for good and bad, it seems that not all Stoics could stick by the austere ideal of considering everything but virtue indifferent, and it is reported that a certain Dionysius of Heraclea abandoned Stoicism because 'owing to the severity of his ophthalmia he had no longer the nerve to call pain a thing indifferent'.[22]

Two distinguished scholars, Martha Nussbaum and Richard Sorabji, have expressed discomfort about the Stoic value theory and attendant disavowal of emotion. Both have sought to retain a broadly Stoic outlook without subscribing to what philosopher Bernard Williams once called 'lethal high-mindedness'. Interestingly, both refer to grief as an example of an emotion that is fully justified in the context of the human commitments that make for a good life (in a non-Stoic sense).

Sorabji has written about 'the unacceptable face of Stoicism' and stated that it is 'better to treat the welfare of our loved ones as something very much more than rightly preferred, even though the Stoics are right that this means incurring the risk of loss and desolation'. He rescues Stoicism by denying that the theory of indifference was indispensable to it, as it 'was not used by Chrysippus as an essential part of this therapy'.[23]

Nussbaum declares herself uneasy with the aspect of Hellenistic ethics that regards a flourishing human life as 'one that has achieved freedom from disturbance and upheaval, above all by reducing the [individual's] commitments to unstable items in the world'.[24] She believes it is possible to detach the useful parts of the Stoic analysis of emotions from the Stoic goal of complete self-sufficiency, which is what she sets out to do in her 'neo-Stoic' approach.

The Stoics are right, Nussbaum says, that emotions are evaluative judgements. They are not necessarily full-blown conscious judgements, as the Stoics believed, though. Instead, they are best seen as a rough and ready form of appraisal. She supports the idea that just like other animals, our own emotions involve the recognition that something is happening in the world that is in some way important for our goals. Even infants make primitive appraisals of this kind. So, emotions are ways of monitoring the relationship between our projects and the environment. They are 'a value-laden way of seeing'.[25]

Nussbaum believes the Stoics are also right that if we value something in the world, something that is not in our full control and is vulnerable to loss, emotions will almost inevitably arise. For instance, it's not possible to believe that someone beloved is lost forever and retain equanimity.[26] She writes:

'To cherish something ... is to give oneself a basis for the response of profound joy when it is present; of fear when it is threatened; of grief when it is lost; of anger when someone else damages it; of envy when someone else has it and you don't; of pity when someone else loses such a thing through no fault of his or her own.'[27]

In that sense, it's true that emotions are expressions of 'neediness and lack of self-sufficiency'.[28] If we allow our well-being to depend at least partly on things in the world that we can't fully control, we do indeed leave ourselves vulnerable to negative emotions.

The question is what we should do with this realisation. For the Stoics, what follows is an exhortation to stop valuing the fragile objects that give rise to emotions. 'The mind without passions is a fortress', says Marcus. 'No place is more secure. Once we take refuge there we are safe forever.'[29] But do we really want our mind to be a fortress, cut off from human emotions and vulnerabilities?

This is where Nussbaum and the Stoics part company. That approach, she writes, is 'excessively violent toward human complexity and frailty'.[30] Instead, she endorses the common-sense view that there are indeed things in the world that are good and bad for our well-being. Banishing the emotions that reflect this would be unwise, as it could lead to a life which is impoverished and less than fully human. A flourishing human life cannot do without some emotional commitments that leave us vulnerable.

The ideal of emotionlessness was already questioned in ancient times. Reflecting on distress, Cicero reports the objections of a philosopher called Crantor:

> 'I cannot by any means agree with those who extol some kind of impassivity. Such a thing is neither possible nor beneficial. I do not wish to be ill, but if I am, and if some part of my body is to be cut open or even amputated, let me feel it. This absence of pain comes at a high price: it means being numb in body, and in mind scarcely human.'[31]

Cicero acknowledges that there is 'some sense' in this. However, he cautions against indulging 'the weak and womanish parts of us', insisting that we 'must resist [the emotions] with all our strength, if we truly wish to spend our allotment of life in peace and tranquility'.[32]

Siding more with Crantor than Cicero, Nussbaum concludes that we can and should care about things like 'health, bodily integrity, work', both our own and those of the people we love. Above all, we can and should care about intimate relationships.[33] But even without the value theory and uncompromising views about emotions, there is still much of relevance in the Stoic literature. For instance, Stoicism can be helpful for countering things like excessive ambition, competitiveness and attachment to worldly goods. We should take seriously the Stoics' invitation to recognise that these hinder rather than help our flourishing.[34]

If, like Nussbaum, we rejected the Stoic theory that virtue is the only good and vice the only evil, we would be free to believe that there are good and bad things in the world apart from virtue and vice. This would open the door to the emotions. If loving relationships were genuinely good and bereavement genuinely bad, our joy at the former and sadness at the latter would not be based on faulty judgements. At least some of our emotions would be appropriate responses to things that are really good and bad, so there would be no reason to try to ban them.

Emotions, however, should be modulated. Aristotle could help us with this task. Rational Emotive Behaviour Therapy (REBT), a form of CBT developed in America in the 1950s, could also be useful. Its founder, Albert Ellis, was partly inspired by Epictetus' idea that it is not *what* happens to us that disturbs us but *how* we react to those things. He shared with the Stoics the ideal of relating to the world more rationally. But in REBT these insights, unhitched from other parts of Stoic theory, are used very differently.

REBT therapist Windy Dryden has written about distinguishing between healthy and unhealthy negative emotions. Healthy emotions are based on rational beliefs, which are *flexible, consistent with reality, logical* and *helpful for pursuing goals and projects*; unhealthy emotions are based on irrational beliefs, which of course are the opposite. In Dryden's scheme, the latter are best replaced with the former: anxiety with concern, for instance; depression with sadness; guilt with remorse, and so on. Like Stoicism, REBT is based on disputing the beliefs associated with our emotions. Unlike Stoicism, in REBT emotions – even anger – can be healthy or unhealthy, depending on the patterns of thought and action associated with them.[35]

Conclusion

In light of all we've looked at in this chapter, I believe that the Stoic ideal needs to be adjusted, resized a bit. Reason, emotion and the body are more intricately connected than the Stoics could have known. We are increasingly understanding how our emotional system evolved as a guide to what we should seek or avoid in order to survive and reproduce. Emotions are extremely valuable, in fact essential, to navigate our transit through the world. Of course, sometimes we can be too afraid, say, or afraid of the wrong thing, but in general fear is a very effective way of alerting us to danger. Without fear, we'd be much more likely to expose ourselves to harm and catastrophe.

True, emotions are not always reliable guides, and we shouldn't always believe them. We're no longer hunter-gatherers and have moved on from the time when our sometimes crude emotional imperatives evolved. Moreover, things can go wrong. Emotions are liable to become detached from environmental stimuli and take on a life of their own, as in depression or anxiety. Nevertheless, it is reasonable to believe that, although we should be wary of being misled by our emotions, much of the time they are decent guides in life, which we ignore at our peril. In fact, brain injuries affecting the areas of the brain that process emotion have been shown to have a negative impact on decision-making.[36]

Even if reason is not the sole good, however, the Stoics rightly draw our attention to how important it is for flourishing. We should exercise our ability to improve ourselves by managing, rather than eradicating, our emotions. While we can accept some worldly things as good or bad, it would seem wise to take up the suggestion to revise our value system and attribute less importance to superficial things like wealth, success and status. At the same time, we need to accept and find ways of dealing with the vulnerability and impermanence of the things we cherish the most.

Chapter 6

MORE THAN HAPPINESS

Picture a smallholder tending a vegetable garden, and a Benedictine monk doing the same thing. On the face of it they are involved in very similar kinds of activities, but in fact their sowing, planting and watering is likely to be guided by two very different notions of flourishing, which the philosopher Charles Taylor has called humanist and transcendent.[1] Humanist flourishing is about leading a good human life, without reference to anything beyond the natural world as we ordinarily understand it. For the smallholder, cultivating the garden is likely to be about producing healthy food for the family, or enjoying working outdoors and being in touch with the rhythms of nature. In the transcendent version, some goods are seen as higher than a good human life; an 'unseen order' (to use William James' phrase), whether or not it is spelled out in terms of a god or an afterlife, takes precedence over *prima facie* human needs. For the monk, cultivating the garden would be primarily about serving God.

Where do Buddhism and Stoicism stand in relation to this distinction between humanist and transcendent flourishing? Since it is possible to downplay the importance of their transcendent aspects, they are both often considered humanist traditions that will help us to live richer lives. But unseen orders feature highly in both, as we have seen in the last two chapters.

Stoicism is a challenging philosophy of over 2,000 years ago, and not all of it translates easily to our times. After all, the modern scientific view is that the universe is utterly indifferent rather than providentially ordered; that our reasoning capacity is the product of evolution and the brain rather than a fragment of divine reason, as confirmed by the fact that brain disease or injury can fundamentally change our character or deprive us of basic cognitive abilities; and that emotions (even negative ones) can be helpful if sometimes problematic guides in life.

As for Buddhism, some of its doctrines might present a challenge if it is our conviction that the only life we have is this one, that science is our best hope for unveiling at least some of the secrets of the universe, and that there's no real escape from the *dukkha* and impermanence that it so aptly brings to our attention.

What do these traditions have to offer a sceptical reader of today? A common approach – if we wish to avoid adopting metaphysics that don't suit a scientifically-informed world-view – is to cherry-pick bits of advice to make us happier or more successful. Take mindfulness. While secular mindfulness-based methods of meditation were originally developed for particular therapeutic purposes, mindfulness is now being claimed to help with all sorts of conventional goals, from making money to spicing up our sex lives to losing weight.

There is nothing wrong with cherry-picking per se. In some sense, that is what I am advocating with this book. The problem is when what's picked only skims the surface of what is on offer.[2] These are demanding traditions that challenge our customary ways of being in the world and the values that ordinarily dominate our lives. Both tell us that the path towards flourishing involves turning our back on the desires and attachments that usually motivate us instead of rushing to satisfy them. To turn Buddhism and Stoicism on their head and use them in the service of an unexamined notion of happiness would be a distortion of their fundamental spirit and a loss.

Rethinking happiness

It may be more fruitful to take the traditions' challenges seriously and to reconsider the meaning and value of happiness. We often distinguish happiness from mere pleasure, but in practice there are large overlaps in the ways we use these terms. For instance, it seems natural to say we are happy when we are enjoying ourselves; conversely, some pleasures are not just fleeting but can provide lasting satisfaction. Similarly, while joy can refer to momentary experiences, joyfulness can also be more of a habitual trait. This lack of clear distinctions is also found in Stoic and Buddhist texts, where translators make different judgements about when to use happiness, pleasure or joy.

At the most basic level, a feeling of pleasure is evolution's reward for some behaviour so that we are motivated to repeat it, just like pain is telling us that something has gone wrong and we should avoid it in the future. But the reward doesn't last, and dissatisfaction never leaves us for too long. So off we go seeking pleasure again, with the same inevitable result. This is the 'hedonic treadmill' we encountered earlier.

According to psychologist Robert Kurzban this is 'evolution's way of keeping the carrot just out of reach, motivating you to continue to do more useful and adaptive things' – for your genes at least.[3] We are the outcome of natural selection, which doesn't 'care' about our well-being, only about our reproductive success: we evolved to survive and reproduce, not to be happy.

But are we compelled to follow the urges instilled in us by evolution? Normally we just follow our desires and anxieties without thinking too much about it. We are constantly, as Bhante Bodhidhamma puts it, 'ricocheting from greed to aversion and back to greed'.[4] However, radical traditions like Buddhism and Stoicism urge us to stop listening to these desires and give up seeking satisfaction through worldly channels. They will not give us what we want. It is only by switching our commitment to the right path that we can reach a different, lasting kind of happiness. So, what do the traditions themselves have to say about this?[5]

I have said that the Greek word *eudaimonia* is often translated as 'happiness' but shouldn't be, since it refers to a more objective sense in which a complete life has been flourishing. Opinions differed about what would facilitate this, but one thing it was never about was just overflowing with jolly feelings and moods.

As should be clear by now, the Stoics equated the good life with a life of virtue and reason. It is natural to want to acquire or avoid other things in the world, but ultimately these are neither good nor bad, and should not be the cause of pleasure or distress. For the Stoics, the kind of happiness we feel about what we perceive as good things happening in the world is just misguided. Things like weddings, babies or promotions, let alone new cars or houses, are outside our control and therefore not appropriate sources of positive feelings of happiness, pleasure or joy. Seneca writes eloquently on this:

> 'Everyone you see is in pursuit of joy, but they do not know where great and lasting joy is to be had. One tries to get it from dinner parties and self-indulgence; another from elections and crowds of supporters; another from his girlfriend; another from pointless display of education and literary studies that do not heal what is amiss. All of them are deceived by specious and short-lived enticements, like drunkenness, that pays for a single hour's cheery insanity with a long-lasting hangover, or like the applause and acclamation of a large following, that costs you great anxiety both to get and to retain.'[6]

Joy based on indifferents could turn into something else at any point, as he explains:

> 'we often say that we are overjoyed that one person was elected consul, or that another was married or that his wife has given birth, events which, far from being causes for joy, are frequently the beginnings of future sorrow.'[7]

There is however one kind of joy the Stoics do approve of, one that 'never ceases or turns into its opposite'.[8] This is felt only about a genuine good, which is virtue: 'the joy that arises from oneself is reliable and strong; it grows; it stays with us right to the end. The other objects that are commonly admired are just goods for the day.'[9] Once we have freed ourselves from desires and fears, 'a huge joy comes in to replace those things that are trivial and fragile and actually prompt self-disgust – a joy unshaken and unvarying, followed by peace and harmony in the mind'.[10]

Such Stoic joy is reserved for the sage, the rare individual who has achieved complete wisdom. For the Stoics, foolish people – which is all of us, pursuing habitual pleasures without due reflection – do not experience true joy any more than the lions who 'rejoice when they have caught their prey'.[11] The sage, and only the sage, can feel a calm joy about being virtuous. This is more like the knowledge that one is thinking and acting in accordance with nature than the zingy feeling we know and love.

Like Stoicism, Buddhism is sceptical about ordinary notions of happiness, what with all the emphasis on the unsatisfactoriness of things. In unison with Seneca, the *Sutta Nipāta* tells us that 'What others speak of as happiness, this the noble ones speak of as misery.'[12]

True, there is much talk of ending suffering. But this means something quite different in Buddhism from how we would ordinarily understand it. We can't eliminate *dukkha* because pain and impermanence are inherent features of existence. All we can hope for is to remove 'the second arrow' – the reactions that make our situation worse – by altering the mind that is experiencing the suffering. If we take 'ending suffering' to mean what we'd all like – to have an existence that is full of delight and completely devoid of pain – then no path leads to it. It is the stuff of fairy tales, not achievable in the real world.

The Buddhist path does welcome certain kinds of happiness, however. Even the Dalai Lama has come out in support. The first sentence of his book *The Art of Happiness* declares: 'I believe that the very purpose of our life is to seek happiness.'[13] Of course, if you read on, it turns out he's not recommending any old pursuit of happiness, of the kind based on chasing desires and the satisfaction of worldly pleasures. Instead, he is talking about training the mind, cultivating contentment and compassion, and developing deep connections with others.

In the *Dhammapāda*, happiness and unhappiness are said to originate in the mind:

> 'Speak or act with a corrupted mind,
> And suffering follows
> As the wagon wheel follows the hoof of the ox.
>
> ...
>
> Speak or act with a peaceful mind,
> And happiness follows
> Like a never-departing shadow.'[14]

According to the texts, just before attaining awakening the Buddha remembered a pleasant experience he'd once had while deep in concentration and realised he didn't have to be wary of such a state:

> 'I thought: "Why am I afraid of that pleasure that has nothing to do with sensual pleasures and unwholesome states?" I thought: "I am not afraid of that pleasure since it has nothing to do with sensual pleasures and unwholesome states."'[15]

The main distinction is between sensual and non-sensual varieties of happiness and pleasure. In Buddhism, happiness based on sensual pleasures is not recommended. In one discourse, the Buddha advises against seeking sensual pleasure, which is said to be 'filthy' and 'coarse'. It is not all proscribed, however, as we learn from this appreciative description of nature: 'the Gosinga Sāla-tree Wood is delightful, the night is moonlit, the *sāla* trees are all in blossom, and heavenly scents seem to be floating in the air.'[16]

Elsewhere the Buddha acknowledges the lure of sensual pleasures but points out that on balance they are problematic, since they are not long-lasting and in the long run cause more suffering than enjoyment.[17] Sensual pleasures are likened to carrying 'a blazing grass torch ... against the wind'. They 'provide much suffering and much despair, while the danger in them is great'.[18] Indulging in sensual gratification also has the undesirable consequence of strengthening the desires that are harmful for us, so that it becomes more and more difficult to turn away from them.

The kind of pleasure that should be cultivated instead is 'the bliss of renunciation, the bliss of seclusion, the bliss of peace, the bliss of enlightenment'.[19] This is a non-sensual, wholesome sort of happiness, which can be gradually refined through ethical conduct, awareness of impermanence and states of concentration.[20]

Ethical conduct

The first form of refined happiness is the bliss we get from ethical conduct. According to the Buddha, if 'defiling states disappear ..., nothing but happiness and delight develops, tranquillity, mindfulness and clear awareness – and that is a happy state'.[21] A wise man is said to be one 'who thinks good thoughts, speaks good words, and does good deeds', and as a result he 'feels pleasure and joy here and now' because he knows he has done no evil.[22]

We may relate to these views more easily if we think of the peacefulness we might feel when we know we're doing the right thing, when although people are being uncooperative and it is unclear how things will turn out, we are satisfied that we've acted properly and done all we could do.

Awareness of impermanence

Counterintuitive though it may sound, joy can also arise from properly understanding impermanence. The Buddha says: 'When, by knowing the impermanence, change, fading away, and cessation of forms, one sees ... with proper wisdom that forms ... are all impermanent, suffering, and subject to change, joy arises.'[23]

Joy can even be evoked by Buddhist death meditations – practices involving contemplation of a corpse and self-reminders that our body is heading for the same fate – which we could imagine to be depressing. This is because such practices are conducive to freedom from the negative mental states associated with being attached to the body.[24] We'll look more closely at death meditations in Chapter 9.

Here we could learn from the Japanese, who have built several art forms and a whole aesthetic on appreciating the essential evanescence of things. This is most famously exemplified in the annual ritual of watching the dazzling but brief blossoming of the cherry trees. Many haiku poems have been written about it. This one is by Issa (1763–1828):

> 'Cherry blossoms in the evening.
> Ah well, today also belongs to the past.'[25]

The ephemeral nature of things should not evoke despair but gratitude for the present moment and a serene sadness at the beauty and fragility of the world.

We can cultivate these feelings simply by attending more carefully to the turning of the seasons. Even in cities we can notice the changing character of sunlight, or the colour of the autumn leaves before they fall.

States of concentration

Finally, some of the *jhāna*s (absorptions) are described as involving states of intense pleasure and happiness that are different from sensual pleasures and unwholesome states.[26] Much like a spring fills every part of a pool with cool water, so too 'the monk suffuses, fills, soaks and drenches this very body with the joy and happiness that come from concentration, so that there is no part of his body that is untouched by that joy and happiness'.[27] Non-sensual pleasure is harnessed as a way of making progress along the path, as non-sensual joy and happiness come to replace the sensual varieties.

Even if we have not experienced high meditative states, we may be able to glimpse this kind of joy by making time for quietly sitting and breathing, allowing our worries to fade into the background, connecting with a fundamental sense of aliveness and well-being.

To sum up, happiness and joy in Buddhism are not a consequence of things like a new romance, or a financial windfall. Rather, they tend to arise as a result of wholesome states, morality and training of the mind through concentration or insight.

Happiness as by-product

If we look beneath the surface, then, Buddhist and Stoic varieties of happiness are not about basking in happy feelings of the common sort. Instead, the traditions champion more reliable and durable forms of happiness. It is important for both that pleasant states of mind are not something to aim for, but a by-product of other things that are good in themselves. Marcus Aurelius reminds himself of this by writing: 'So were you born to feel "nice"?'[28] Although Seneca and Epictetus sometimes give the impression that tranquillity is the aim, overall they clearly espouse the Stoic view that the goal is a life in agreement with nature, which brings with it a state of tranquillity – not the other way around.

Seneca explains this with a poetic simile:

'Just as in a field that has been plowed for corn some flowers grow up in between, yet all that work was not undertaken for this little plant, however much it pleases the eyes ... so too, pleasure is not the reward or the motive of virtue but an accessory'.[29]

The proper sources of joy and happiness are fundamental in one formulation of the Buddhist path found in the early texts. This consists of *sīla* (ethical action or morality), *samādhi* (concentration or meditation) and *pañña* (insight, understanding or wisdom).[30] These three elements build on each other and are to be developed together. It has been argued that, among these three, morality and insight are the essential elements of the ultimate goal, while meditation is mainly a way to cultivate those.[31]

The interconnection of insight and ethical action is also in evidence in the most famous formulation of the Buddhist way, the noble eightfold path (right view, right intention, right speech, right action, right livelihood, right effort, right mindfulness, right concentration) – a holistic system in which the cognitive elements cannot be separated from the practical and ethical ones.[32]

A number of texts and commentators put ethics and insight together at the heart of the Buddhist path. The twentieth-century Buddhist monk and scholar Walpola Rahula writes that in the Buddhist way of life 'wisdom and compassion' (which also stands for qualities like love, charity, kindness, tolerance) are inextricably linked.[33] One discourse portrays a symbiotic relationship between wisdom/insight and ethical conduct: just like two hands washing each other, 'wisdom is purified by morality, and morality is purified by wisdom: where one is, the other is, the moral man has wisdom and the wise man has morality, and the combination of morality and wisdom is called the highest thing in the world'.[34]

The parallel with Stoicism here is striking. Seneca writes about the connection between insight and ethical action in a similar tone: 'An action will not be right unless one's intention is right, since that is the source of the action. This intention will not be right, in its turn, unless the mental disposition is right, since that is the source of the intention. Further, the mental disposition will not be optimal unless the person has ... brought the truth to bear on his situation.'[35]

In Buddhism, morality and wisdom are cultivated gradually. The path starts with the former, but it is not linear, and the two build on each other.[36] Just as insight is necessary to be clear about the right thing to do, similarly beginning to shed egocentric and unwholesome attitudes can help us to develop clarity of understanding.

How does the third limb of the path, *samādhi*, fit in with ethical action and insight? The term occurs with very broad meanings in the texts. Although it leans heavily towards concentration, it could also be translated as meditation.[37] But the English word 'meditation' is ambiguous, and a broader translation is put forward by Rahula, who understands *samādhi* as 'mental discipline'.[38]

There is also in the texts a more general idea of development or cultivation (*bhāvanā*).[39] As Buddhist studies scholar Rupert Gethin puts it, this refers to 'mental or spiritual exercises aimed at developing and cultivating wholesome mental states that conduce to the realization of the Buddhist path'.[40] Alongside meditative practices, these exercises include reading, reciting and transmitting the texts. For Rahula, study and discussion of certain topics are actually forms of meditation.[41] According to Richard Gombrich, the methods employed included cultivating the imagination and the use of reason.[42] These intellectual aspects of Buddhist training are often overlooked.

Is there anything in Stoicism that parallels this? Actually, there is. Stoic practice involved 'mental or spiritual exercises' (*askēsis*) to bring the doctrines to life, such as memorising passages, doing visualisations and practical exercises. The aim is to be ready to respond appropriately to whatever life throws at us, no matter how challenging.

There is much that we can learn from this. We take reading for granted, but if we thought of it as a kind of meditation, as part of our spiritual training, we could engage with it in a way that helps us to grow in wisdom. For instance, we could choose a text that inspires us and read from it every day, reflecting on its implications for how we conduct our daily life.

For all their differences, there seems to be a large overlap between the two traditions' spiritual exercises – both challenge normal habits of thought and behaviour and promote awareness, ethical development, non-reactivity, and intellectual or meditative understanding.

Conclusion

Both Buddhism and Stoicism strongly encourage us to cultivate *understanding* and *ethical action* through *spiritual practice*. We may not share their precise views, but they certainly seem correct in their assessment that a good life requires more than positive feelings. A life filled with nothing but drug-induced bliss could never count as a good human life, as we would not have even begun to develop the qualities that make us human.

This is not to say there is no place in a good life for ordinary joy and happiness. But the happiness of a new relationship, or an exciting holiday, while welcome when it comes along, is dependent on things outside ourselves going well, things that are impermanent and mostly not in our control.

It is therefore a vulnerable, unreliable state that should be accepted as such and not given excessive importance.

The traditions are also right in pointing to understanding, ethical action and self-development as important elements of a good life. A life that contains all three is good in itself, but it is also more likely to produce a well-being that is deeper and more stable than any fleeting and unreliable feelings of pleasure based on delusions and distant chimeras. In the next three chapters I will look at these interconnected topics, which could be at the centre of a modern practice.

Chapter 7

REMOVING THE DUST
FROM OUR EYES

Just after his awakening, the Buddha was disinclined to teach, feeling that his generation delighted in attachment and wouldn't be receptive to his message. Then the god Brahmā Sahampati intervened. Pleading that there were some 'with little dust in their eyes', who would understand and benefit from the Buddha's teaching, the god persuaded him to change his mind.[1] So the Buddha resolved to share his insight with those on earth who were not completely deluded and would listen to what he had to say.

Seeing clearly

In both Buddhism and Stoicism, seeing things clearly is crucial. As we have seen, it is mainly wrong views about the world that send us chasing satisfaction in treacherous directions.

For the Stoics, wrong views are the faulty judgements that lead us to value things other than reason and virtue, and in so doing give rise to emotions. The impressions we need to challenge are not basic ones, like that it's raining or that a car is coming towards us (although we may well make mistakes about that kind of thing if we're intoxicated or feeling unwell). Rather, we need to question the evaluations of good and bad that, limpet-like, attach themselves to our perceptions. For example, when we think that love or people's approval are important in life, emotions immediately appear: we feel joyful that we've found love or proud that people respect us, then upset if love is lost or approval withdrawn.

Buddhist attitudes about views are complicated. Some passages suggest a radically sceptical philosophy that advocates taking no view at all. The monk who is at peace 'does not take up or discard any view – he has shaken them all off', say some verses considered among the oldest in the Canon.[2] But in general the texts draw a clear enough distinction between right and wrong view.[3] There are even lists of wrong views. One discourse notes 62 kinds, mostly speculations about the eternity or infinity of self and world, or about past and future.[4] Some wrong views are more down to earth, as in the case of a monk called Ariṭṭha, who formed the 'pernicious view' that there would be no harm in a monk having sexual intercourse with a woman. The Buddha reminded the monks in no uncertain terms of the right view: 'that one can engage in sensual pleasures, without sensual desires, without perceptions of sensual desire, without thoughts of sensual desire – that is impossible.'[5]

It is probably safe to say that in Buddhism failing to see the truths of *dukkha*, impermanence and not-self is pretty seriously wrong. The four distortions of perception, thought or view (see p. 35) set us straight on this, reminding us how misconceived it is to perceive impermanent things as permanent, find pleasure in *dukkha* and see self where there is no self.

But it is not just the *content* of our views that can be right or wrong. Attachment to views, like any other attachment, is not a good thing. 'Right view' does not mean only subscribing to certain understandings of human life and the world, but also holding them with the right *attitude*. Even right views need to be held undogmatically.

This seems like sound advice. In order to dislodge dogmatism, it is a good idea to remind ourselves that even things that seem obvious to us are often disputed by others. We can practise questioning our beliefs, asking what reasons there might be to doubt them, or why sensible people might disagree with us.

However, there is a more dogmatic streak running through both traditions. Although they both encourage thinking things through and testing beliefs, in practice they also often rely on handed-down doctrines that would simply have to be accepted. According to the French ancient philosophy scholar Pierre Hadot: 'The dogmas and methodological principles of [Hellenistic schools, including Stoicism] are not open to discussion. In this period, to philosophize is to choose a school, convert to its way of life, and accept its dogmas.'[6]

Even the *Kālāma Sutta*, often cited with keen enthusiasm as containing the advice to test doctrines against one's own experience instead of relying on tradition or authority, may not be quite what it seems. The American Buddhist monk and translator Bhikkhu Bodhi writes that there is an interesting discrepancy between this advice and that offered in the Chinese version of the discourse, according to which the Buddha instead tells his audience: 'You yourselves do not have pure wisdom to know which deeds are transgressions and which are not transgressions.'[7]

Regardless of whether or not there is a tension within the traditions between dogmatism and open-mindedness, both were ultimately optimistic about our ability to see clearly. This involves learning to mistrust ordinary perceptions and ceasing to overvalue items that are impermanent and outside our control. With guidance and practice, we can come out of the fog and into clear sunshine.

Is this optimistic view of our capacities completely justified? There are reasons to be hesitant. Our knowledge of the way the human mind has evolved shows that survival does not always rely on making truthful judgements. Sometimes accurate information is important for survival and reproduction, sometimes it isn't. In assessing danger, it's better to be more sensitive and less accurate than the opposite: for instance, frequently mistaking things that resemble snakes is a price worth paying for being alert enough to spot a real one.

The obstacles to a 20/20 vision of the truth do not delegitimise the entire enterprise of trying to see at least a little more clearly. But do we have reason to believe that Buddhists and Stoics might be pointing us in a more truthful direction when they challenge our everyday sense that worldly goods are valuable and worth pursuing, or that we are a separate and solid 'self'? Let's look at each of these challenges.

Rejecting worldly values

Both Buddhism and Stoicism rejected the pre-eminence of worldly values, goals and beliefs, although both cautioned against pushing such rejection to the extreme forms it sometimes took in their contemporary societies. In several discourses the Buddha condemns in colourful terms the extreme asceticism he had misguidedly pursued before his awakening, and through which his backside had become 'like a camel's hoof', his scalp 'shrivelled and withered as a green bitter gourd shrivels and withers in the wind and sun'.[8]

The Stoics also emerged from a culture in which extreme asceticism had its devotees. After all, the seeds of their ideas began to sprout in the midst of the Cynic school, for which living in accordance with nature meant rejecting conventional customs and all aims like wealth, property and reputation. Diogenes Laertius, for instance, tells us that the Cynic Diogenes of Sinope lived in a barrel in the marketplace and ate raw meat (although he also tells us that Diogenes was not able to digest it).[9] But while the Stoics retained some Cynic views, they didn't advocate such antics.

Despite these rejections of extremism, the overall message of both Buddhism and Stoicism is clearly one of renunciation. The suspicion is not just of food, drink, sex and other pleasures of the senses. It's equally about all sorts of other things in which we tend to get caught up: social standing, other people's respect and admiration, wealth, climbing the career ladder. In Buddhist terms, these are just as *dukkha* and impermanent. In Stoic terms, they are just as outside our control.

Generally, Stoic philosophers were not overly impressed by our physicality. Epictetus advises to 'treat your whole body as a poor heavily-loaded ass', while Seneca describes the body as 'a listless and unhealthy animal'. A 'clean and seemly' one, mind, who deserves clean clothing, but still an animal.[10]

The idea is not to neglect our body. Like a horse that has been entrusted to our care, Epictetus says we should wash it, 'rub it, take care that no one turns away from it or is disgusted by it'.[11] But we can choose whether to prioritise our animal or divine nature, and if we want to be god-like we should give pride of place to our mind, treating the body as unimportant.[12]

As for material goods, Epictetus tells us to 'take only what you absolutely need in relation to meat, drink, clothing, house, household slaves. But reject everything that is for show and luxury.'[13] It is interesting to note that a small number of household slaves might have counted as a need in the culture of the time. Still, we get the point.

According to Musonius Rufus, thoughtless people seek rare and expensive items because they confuse what is genuinely good and noble with what is only apparently so, 'just as insane people confuse black things with white'.[14] Food should be for nourishment and sex for procreation, neither for pleasure. Our dress should be 'modest, not expensive and excessive', and hair 'cut to remove the excess, not to become elegant'. We must avoid luxurious living, which fosters greed. He himself would 'choose to be sick rather than to live in luxury. Being sick harms the body only; living in luxury harms both soul and body'.[15]

Similarly, Seneca writes that we should resist our inclination to seek things like wealth, pleasures, beauty and ambition, or avoid 'hard physical work, death, pain, public disapproval, and an austere diet'.[16] Musonius sums it all up it nicely by saying that 'one man and one man only is truly wealthy – he who learns to want nothing in every circumstance.'[17]

Seneca did try to reconcile Stoicism with wealth. Already from a rich family, he accumulated large sums under the notorious emperor Nero, to whom he was tutor, and ended up owning vast areas of land and property, becoming fabulously rich. In 'On the Happy Life', he begins, as we might expect from a Stoic, by pointing out that material goods and riches are 'shiny on the outside, but on the inside are pitiful'.[18] But in the same work he repeatedly defends wealth, writing that no one 'has sentenced wisdom to poverty' and that the wise person 'does not love wealth, but he does prefer it'.[19] Elsewhere, he writes that such indifferents are fine so long as we don't get excessively attached to them, which again is a standard Stoic position: 'May all those things come to us, but may they not cling to us; so that if they should be taken away, their departure will not tear us apart.'[20]

In Buddhism, likewise, there is an important difference between enjoying something and being attached to it. But in practice it may be really quite difficult to stop one from sliding into the other. And reading between the lines it seems that reconciling the two points of view was a bit of a struggle for Seneca. He was accused of hypocrisy and profiting from usury, and he never completely cleared the issue of the morally corrupting effect of accepting huge sums from a dubious character like Nero.

No doubt Seneca tried to square these things, reassure himself that he was doing what he could in exacting circumstances. In the end, though, he had to admit that he was not really living up to his ideals: 'I am not wise, and ... I will not be wise. Demand from me, then, not that I am equal to the best but that I am better than the bad.'[21]

Later in life, Seneca made more consistent pronouncements about the false promises of wealth: 'Money never made
anyone rich: all it does is infect everyone who touches it with
a lust for more of itself.'[22] He yearned for a life of quiet contemplation. He attempted to give Nero his wealth back but was
rebuffed. Maybe there is a right way for a Stoic to be rich, but
it looks like Seneca never found it.[23]

The Stoics may not always have lived up to their high ideals, and we may not agree with everything they advise, but we
can take from them the useful habit of checking our values. We
can ask ourselves: what makes us truly rich? How important is
reputation, really? Are we too dependent on others' approval
and admiration? Or hooked on comfort?

The Buddha, for his part, talks about the 'eight worldly
conditions' that 'keep the world turning around', and around
which the world turns. 'What eight? Gain and loss, fame and
disrepute, praise and blame, pleasure and pain'.[24]

An untrained person takes these at face value and is consumed by them, elated at gains or people's approval, dejected
about pain or loss of status. A trained disciple, on the other
hand, is able to see through these as *dukkha* and impermanent,
therefore is neither dazzled by gain, fame, praise or pleasure,
nor unduly distressed by loss, disrepute, blame and pain. 'The
way to material gain is one thing,' warns the *Dhammapāda*, 'the
path to Nirvana another.'[25]

Reclaiming (some) worldly values

Both Buddhism and Stoicism imply, if not explicitly advocate,
a negative appraisal of our animal nature. The body and bodily
matters, as well as common objects of desire such as success

and wealth, are downgraded. While neither tradition favours an intransigent ascetic position that demands we renounce basic human needs, both are radical enough to tell us that what we normally find valuable, the goals we normally pursue, the paths we normally take through life, are not as worthwhile as we think.

Mistaken about good and bad, unwittingly taken in by things that are ultimately harmful for us, we suffer from something akin to a perceptual illusion, only much deeper and more problematic. It's like the Müller-Lyer illusion: we can't help experiencing the lines as of different length, even if we know they're not.

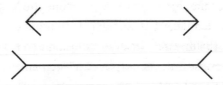

In a similar way, faulty ways of understanding are cognitive illusions. These can't be easily overcome; all we can do is become familiar with them and learn to catch them as best we can. In a way, both Buddhism and Stoicism tell us that most of what we value and desire is a kind of cognitive illusion, and their strategy is similar: to become more aware of these illusions so we can resist their lure. The question is to what extent we should agree with this assessment if we have let go of some of the traditional views described in previous chapters. The answer wholly depends on how we conceive of ourselves as human beings.

We have to start from where we are, and what we basically are is creatures moulded by evolution. We are animals, therefore subject to all the urges and impulses that prod animals' behaviour. These evolved to face the challenges that, if met, would secure survival and reproduction. Psychologists Kenrick and Griskevicius have counted seven of these: 'evading physical harm, avoiding disease, making friends, gaining status, attracting a mate, keeping that mate, and caring for family.'[26]

These challenges were so important that natural selection threw up the mechanism of pleasurable and painful feelings to make us pursue the things that from the point of view of survival were good for us, like feeding ourselves and mating, and avoid those that were bad for us, like predators and disease. From unknown neural algorithms, feelings pop up that lead us towards the former and away from the latter.

We also have features that we don't share with non-human animals. Without trying to be too exact, we can at least say that as far as we know only we are capable of thinking about things that could have happened, or that might be but are not. We can reason about a prospective course of action and decide whether to go for it or get away quickly. We can communicate with each other about this in precise detail. We are able to extend our feelings of empathy from kin and immediate affiliates to wider circles, even the whole of humanity.

We are rational animals, creatures of mind and body, not reducible to one or the other. But through the evolutionary lens we can identify only what sorts of things we evolved to seek and want, not whether or to what extent we should endorse them now. Fight or flight responses that served us well in the wild, for instance, may be unhelpful if we work in an office. We have to think it all through for ourselves.

Natural selection prompts us to fulfil our desires. Largely ignoring these prompts is what Buddhism and Stoicism and other wisdom traditions ask us to do, telling us that is not the way.[27] Which should we follow? Do we actually need what we evolved to desire?

One way of trying to get to grips with this is by distinguishing between what we need and what we want. But making this distinction work is more difficult than we might think. What are our needs, really? In order to survive we need food, water and shelter. That's it. In order to flourish we need more. Even hard-core ascetics, who have pared down their needs to the minimum, would have a commitment to a set of values, or a project, that provides them with more than the basics of survival.

But the 'something more' needed for a meaningful life is slippery and hard to capture. Does Maslow's hierarchy of safety, belonging, respect and self-fulfilment cover the range of human needs?[28] One difficulty is that just because something is a natural, strongly and widely held desire, it doesn't automatically mean it's a need. As many spiritual traditions point out, there is scope for challenging our perception of need. Needs are to a large extent elastic.

Philosopher Emrys Westacott writes that 'the notion of "basic needs" is unstable because it is historically and culturally relative'. Living a simple life has become harder: things that were once luxuries, like hot running water or a phone, are nowadays considered necessities. He also reminds us that it is not just about material possessions. Compared with the ancient world we have access to a huge range of recreational opportunities, and 'many are forms of consumption that require money'.[29]

In practice therefore we each have to decide for ourselves what our needs are, bearing in mind that when we feel we need something it doesn't mean we actually do. It may be that we just really, really want it. We would all benefit from honestly questioning ourselves about this.

Aristotle's discussion of what a good life requires is worth consulting here, as for balance and clarity it is still hard to beat. Very briefly, his conclusions are:

- Bodily pleasures have a place in the good life, but in moderation. Too much focus on them leads people to live lives 'that are fit only for cattle'. Generally, pleasures that result from engaging in study or worthwhile activity are preferable.[30]

- Money matters but should not be too central a goal, as it's only a means to an end. We 'can act in accordance with virtue even from modest resources'. The wise person is like a shoemaker who 'makes the noblest shoe out of the leather he is given'.[31]

- Success and fame should not be given too much importance, as they are too dependent on unreliable external factors falling into place, and anyway, we don't just want to be honoured, we want to be honoured by people we respect and for good reasons.

- Human relationships are essential to flourishing: 'No one would choose to live without friends, even if he had all the other goods'. There are different degrees of friendship, and the most significant ones are those based on mutual respect.[32]

• The most important ingredient of a good life is activity involving reason, which is most defining of a human being.[33] While reason must be uppermost in a fully human life, we should also take care of our more biological needs, since 'human nature is not self-sufficient for contemplation, but the body must be healthy and provided with food and other care'.[34] This much the Stoics acknowledged. Reading Aristotle, we could come to the stronger conclusion that even though reason is the most distinctive human feature, a rich human life should fully accommodate, not just tolerate, aspects of our animal nature and the emotions. Famously, unlike the Stoics, Aristotle called for their moderation rather than eradication. It is *inappropriate* emotions and *excessive* attachments that we should endeavour to change.[35]

Aristotle was also closer to our modern sensibility by being less sanguine about death, going as far as saying that the more flourishing someone's life is, 'the more pain he will feel at the thought of death. For life is especially worth living for a person like this, and he knows that he is losing the greatest goods – and this is painful.'[36]

But even if death *is* an evil, it is one we can't do anything about. Epicurus said that 'Against all else it is possible to provide security, but as against death all of us mortals alike dwell in an unfortified city.'[37] In this respect we'd be wise to follow Buddhists and Stoics and really accept that, like everything else, our bodies and the bodies of those we love are subject to ageing and decay, instead of feeling, when we fall ill or suffer a bereavement, that someone somewhere must have singled us out for especially bad treatment.

In Stoicism and Buddhism, allowing any worldly needs or pleasures to play a significant role in the good life means attaching ourselves too closely to the impermanent things of the world, making ourselves vulnerable to their loss.[38] More in the spirit of Aristotle, we might decide we'd rather live fully in the world than seek invulnerability. Living fully in the world would include allowing ourselves a moderate enjoyment of the pleasures that come with our embodied nature. Here we could adopt Epicurus' advice that: 'No pleasure is itself evil, but the things which produce certain pleasures entail annoyances many times greater than the pleasures themselves.'[39] Some pleasures are addictive or have harmful consequences, so we should watch out.

But that wouldn't stop us agreeing with Buddhists and Stoics that we are to a large extent mistaken about the value of certain things. It does seem like a good idea to remind ourselves that it's foolish to identify happiness with the satisfaction of our next desire, to chase it by stepping on the hedonic treadmill. We do not have to reject all worldly goods to avoid being consumed by desire for them or by fears about not having them. Wealth, status and appearance are overvalued, and we should cut them to size. This means challenging habits of acquisitiveness, and reducing our attachment to material possessions and conventional goals.

Research has corroborated this, showing that a 'materialistic value orientation' – which does not mean having things per se, but believing that status, money and possessions will make us happy – is linked to lower subjective well-being, more negative self-appraisal and physical and mental health problems (particularly depression and anxiety).[40]

But when it comes to more essential worldly goods, we should be careful about putting too much emphasis on the 'indifferent' side of the Stoic 'preferred indifferent'. While love, friendship, health and life itself are all impermanent and to a large extent outside our control, there is no reason why their transience should call their importance into question. Denying their value might spare us some suffering but at too high a cost. Perhaps no-suffering can only be a corollary of nothing-much-valued, and that's not a good way to live. Instead, our task is to come to terms with the ephemeral nature of those things, with the fact they can be snatched away from us at any time, that they will be often unattainable or lost, and there's not much we can do other than accept it.

The self

Our sense that we are a self authoring our actions and persisting through time is a wrong view in Buddhism. It is a kind of delusion that originates in failing to see that 'self' is only a label referring to a collection of shifting phenomena. Our experience of 'self' in fact breaks down into five main mental and physical components, or aggregates. As we saw on pages 23–4, these are: bodily phenomena; feelings; cognitions; volitional activities; and consciousness.

It's not too difficult to come to share this or a similar analysis. It is undeniable after all that if we 'look inside' we become aware of different experiences but consistently fail to encounter a 'self'. As many have remarked, when we start paying close attention, the self just vanishes. This challenge to the conventional perception of a discrete self inhabiting our brain, thinking our thoughts and feeling our feelings, resonates with modern scientific views that there is no one centre of consciousness or control in the brain.

For instance, Kurzban's theory describes the human mind as made up of lots of separate, interacting 'modules' – little 'selves', in a way, colourfully likened to iPhone apps.[41] Modules, or 'sub-selves', each process different kinds of information and perform specific functions. (They needn't have any particular spatial location in the brain.) They evolved for different purposes, therefore have different priorities. Sometimes they chime, sometimes they are at odds or in competition with each other. At times one is in charge, at times another. This is why we are so complicated, plagued by so many contradictions.[42] A lot of these conflicts are between 'impatient' modules and those with an eye on the future: one module wants to eat ice-cream now, another is more interested in long-term health, and reconciling them can be difficult.

If the mind is made up of all these disparate modules, which may or may not be in communication with each other, there arises the need for one of them to speak for all. This is what we perceive as 'I'. It is through this module, which appears to be in charge, that we have conscious awareness of the world. The disturbing thing is that this 'I' has only limited access to cognitive processes, which for the most part keep doing their own thing quietly out of consciousness. 'We' may think we're doing something for a certain reason, while all the time our decision was caused by something completely different.[43]

But the sense of a self that is in charge is so captivating that we continue to mistake the small conscious part we call 'I' for who we are, even if we have become fully aware that by far the largest part of us lies submerged in our unknowable unconscious depths.

In this theory, the conscious module is much more about PR and spin doctoring than about control. The story goes like this: our survival depends on communication with others. We need others to need and like us. This is why it is of the utmost importance to present ourselves in the best possible way that is still plausible. To that end, not only is truth unnecessary, but it may sometimes be advantageous to act under a certain amount of misinformation.[44]

The many distortions revealed by recent research – believing we have more favourable traits than is realistic, for instance, or overestimating our control over outcomes, or being more optimistic about the future than is justified – may therefore not be errors at all, but instead have a clear and specific function.[45] If we view ourselves through rose-tinted glasses, inflating our positive traits and qualities, others are more likely to see us in a positive light too. If we believe we are more competent than we are, for instance, we are more likely to persuade an interview panel to employ us.

Whether or not we choose to use the language of modules, nowadays most psychologists and neuroscientists would support the view that the mind is fragmented and breaks down into subroutines with different functions. There is no place in the brain where conscious experience comes together. Instead, all kinds of mental activity happen in parallel: some of it will become conscious and some won't; some will leave traces and some won't. The sense of having a unified self is created by the mind concocting a coherent story in which all these processes belong to the same 'I'.[46]

In Buddhism, the false belief in a separate, lasting self is connected not only with ignorance but also with greed and attachment, and so with the ethical sphere. This is why overcoming the delusion of separateness can open up the possibility of genuine generosity and compassion.[47] The idea is that if we stop clinging to thoughts, moods and desires as 'ours'; if we realise there are no sharp divisions between self and other; and if we understand how closely connected our flourishing is to other people's, we will realise that their welfare is as important as our own. Once again, this is not only a question of intellectual understanding but of a transformed life experience.

Is this revised view of self a way of seeing more clearly? The answer seems to be yes. There is no reason to believe in an eternal soul, while there is good reason to think that the basis of self is the biological brain, which is clearly impermanent.[48]

This doesn't mean we're wrong to experience ourselves as 'selves'. On an everyday level, away from meditative experiences that may reveal otherwise hidden vistas, our sense of there being an inner 'me' that endures seems pretty inescapable. This might not be so bad: without an ordinary sense of self it wouldn't be possible to function in the world, and even the Buddha had to be able to do that.[49] But it's worth remembering that ultimately our self is not what it seems. This could help us to accept our mortality and loosen our view of ourselves, preventing us from getting trapped into an excessively rigid notion of who we are.

At first sight the Stoic soul appears far removed from the Buddhist understanding of self. As we have seen, for the Stoics the soul was a fragment of God. It was unitary, meaning that there was no inner conflict; the fact that we do experience such internal division was explained through quick shifts of opinion.[50] But there may be more overlap than it seems. The Stoic ideal of living in accordance with nature can be interpreted as a kind of self-transcendence, as coming to see oneself not as an isolated entity but a small part of a larger continuum.[51] This seems akin to what Sam Harris, in relation to Buddhism, has described as losing 'one's sense of being a separate self' and experiencing a 'boundless, open awareness'.[52]

Conclusion

There is much truth behind the traditional doctrines. All worldly things are *dukkha*, impermanent, not-self; they are outside our control. We need to accept this. We'd all benefit from taking a more detached view of our objects of desire. Some things – especially those that we feel pressurised to achieve because of their social currency, like wealth and success – may not be worth pursuing too vigorously or putting at the centre of our life.

As the traditions suggest, we should work on reconciling ourselves with the fact that everything will come to an end, including ourselves. This is true even if we have concluded that things which are impermanent and not in our control can be valuable. We don't have to pretend that nothing bad has happened if we suffer a serious illness or a bereavement.

It is open to us to be more objective and to reach behind the illusory surface of things to some extent – to remove at least some of the dust from our eyes. But we should revise the ancients' exhortations to see clearly, embracing the value of knowledge and understanding whether or not our conclusions turn out to be in agreement with specific Buddhist or Stoic doctrines. This means, first of all, trying to understand what a good life requires in the context of a meaningless universe, in which there is no ultimate purpose and any meaning to be had is self-created.

A commitment to thinking and seeing as clearly as we can involves cultivating qualities and dispositions like curiosity, awareness, reflection and intellectual honesty; valuing reason and evidence; and testing our own views and countering innate biases to the best of our ability. It might also mean cultivating a healthy scepticism about finding out what things are really like. Marcus himself admitted that 'Things are wrapped in such a veil of mystery that many good philosophers have found it impossible to make sense of them.'[53] Sometimes, the only sound thing to do is to suspend judgement.

Ethical action is the other side of the seeing clearly coin. If we see things clearly we will be more inclined to act rightly, through an awareness of how interconnected all lives are. On the other hand, acting rightly and beginning to overcome self-centredness will help us to see more clearly, by removing the blinkers of self-absorption that normally limit our view of the world. It's now time to look at the ethical side of that coin.

Chapter 8

THE SAGE AND
THE BUDDHA:
MODELS FOR LIVING

We've already seen how the story of the Buddha's awakening illustrates the importance of seeing clearly. It also demonstrates the centrality of compassion, as the Buddha's decision to share his insights was motivated by compassion for the suffering world.[1] The Buddhist path is built on both understanding and ethics.

In the streamlined formulation of the path that we looked at earlier – *sīla, samādhi, paññā* (ethical action or morality, concentration or meditation, and wisdom or insight) – ethics is indispensable. According to the *Dhammapāda*, the core principles of the path are ethical: 'Doing no evil, Engaging in what's [wholesome], And purifying one's mind: This is the teaching of the buddhas.'[2]

In Stoicism, living well is synonymous with living rationally, which is synonymous with virtue. We are predisposed to act ethically and would always do so if we didn't get corrupted by external factors. 'Each and every one of us ... is disposed by nature to live without error and honourably', says Musonius Rufus.[3]

Moral value is grounded in the obscure, elusive concept of *oikeiōsis*. This refers to something like a sense of affinity, or being well-disposed towards something. It first finds expression through a kind of self-concern, an instinct of self-preservation that all animals including humans have and that leads them to seek what is beneficial and avoid what is harmful, according to their different natures. For non-human animals this involves things like finding food and water and avoiding predators. But for beings whose essential nature is reason, such as ourselves, preserving rationality (which is the same as cultivating virtue) is even more important. This is why, in certain circumstances, it's rational for us to choose death over doing something wrong, like betraying a friend, or flattering a tyrant.[4]

This ethical concern takes us beyond animal self-preservation. Because our lives are all intertwined, we would be wrong to seek our good in isolation from other human beings. As we grow up we come to recognise this and expand the sphere of our 'natural concern'.

Both Buddhism and Stoicism have ethics at their core and encourage us to make it a central part of our lives. But what does it mean to be ethical?

Perfectionism

Both traditions set a very high ethical bar. There is an ocean of difference between those who have become truly virtuous, or awakened, and the rest of us, even those who are moved by good intentions.

In Buddhism, as we have seen (p. 52), in attaining nir-vana the *arahant* extinguishes the three unwholesome roots – greed, aversion and delusion – and is motivated only by their opposites: *non-attachment, kindness* and *wisdom*. One discourse says that the Buddha 'has abandoned all unwholesome states and possesses wholesome states'.[5]

It is said that an *arahant* is incapable of doing nine things: 1. 'deliberately taking the life of a living being'; 2. 'taking what is not given'; 3. 'having sexual intercourse'; 4. 'telling a deliber-ate lie'; 5. 'storing up goods for sensual indulgence'; and acting wrongly through 6. attachment, 7. hatred, 8. folly, and 9. fear.[6]

In another discourse the Buddha talks about the supremely accomplished ascetic being 'beyond training'. This kind of talk has sometimes been interpreted as meaning that the *arahant* is beyond morality. In fact, the opposite is the case: morality has become internalised to the point that wholesome actions always flow naturally.[7] In a way, the *arahant* cannot but act morally.

In Stoicism, too, the sage is unable to do the wrong thing. All the sage's actions are virtuous, with vicious impulses com-pletely absent. The virtue of sages is infallible. They have fully internalised right reason, and this means their moral judge-ments are always entirely correct. Sages always know what to do. They are, in fact, a little like gods.[8]

It's not cheery news for everybody else though, since for the Stoics there are no degrees of virtue, and apart from the sage we are all 'utterly wicked'.[9] What are the rest of us to do? One thing we could do is look to the sage for guidance. There are two problems with this: one is that, although exceptional figures like Socrates were held up as exemplars by the Stoics, sages are a bit thin on the ground – in fact they are 'as rare as the phoenix'.[10]

The other problem is that even if we knew what virtuous action the sage would perform in a particular situation, and wanted to reproduce it, *our* action would not be virtuous. This is because the sage acts from a completely consistent virtuous disposition, and we don't. We might perform an externally identical action, even based on the very same intention – we might help a needy person on an altruistic impulse, for instance – but our action would still not be virtuous, as it wouldn't have arisen from the same kind of disposition.

Virtue is beyond us because it involves a settled pattern of motivation and action, and we could never act from that place ourselves. All we can do is use reason to acquire the right views and follow this up by doing the right thing more and more often, encouraging ourselves to acquire the right habits and dispositions.

The Stoics did have a category of those who are 'making progress', but strictly speaking the progressor was still foolish. Chrysippus used the analogy of a man drowning:

> 'Just as in the sea the man a cubit from the surface is drowning no less than the one who has sunk 500 fathoms, so neither are they any the less in vice who are approaching virtue than they who are a long way from it ... so those who are "making progress" continue to be stupid and depraved until they have attained virtue.'[11]

On the other hand, progress towards virtue is within our reach. It is not possible to be faultless, says Epictetus, 'but it is possible to endeavour constantly to be without fault'.[12]

The Buddha is also positive about the possibility of gradual progress:

'I do not say that final knowledge is achieved all at once. On the contrary, final knowledge is achieved by gradual training, by gradual practice, by gradual progress.'[13]

Both traditions hold a lofty ideal of an individual who has developed perfect spontaneous morality. While this may be next to unachievable for ordinary humans, we can be heartened by the possibility of improvement. We have to start somewhere. Using Stoic terminology, we could draw a useful distinction between virtue, which equates to perfected agency, and virtuous activity, which is a matter of degree.[14]

One way to cultivate such virtuous activity could be to adapt Benjamin Franklin's famous self-improvement programme. Franklin made a list of the virtues he believed were most important, focusing on one each week. He kept a kind of scorecard on which he daily marked every time he failed to exhibit a virtue. We could make a similar list of cherished virtues, but might find it more useful to concentrate on the positives, noticing when we succeed as well as when we fail.

Apart from looking to the accomplished ones for inspiration, what ethical guidance is there for the as yet unvirtuous or unenlightened?

Precepts

In Buddhism, there are different levels of ethical teachings. The basic rules for good conduct are set out in the precepts.

There are five precepts for lay people and rather more for monks. For lay people, the precepts advise refraining from:

1. harming living creatures
2. taking what is not given
3. sexual misconduct
4. false speech
5. taking intoxicants that cause heedlessness.

In certain circumstances, lay people might commit themselves to eight precepts. In these, the third precept is replaced with abstaining from all sexual behaviour; they also add refraining from eating after midday, attending entertainments, or using perfumes and luxurious beds. For monastics, a discourse comprehensively sets out the actions to undertake or avoid, down to, among other things, abstaining from injuring seeds and plants, wearing garlands, or accepting goats, sheep, fowl, pigs and other animals.[15]

Precepts are useful when first entering the path, but their potential downside is an excessive attachment to rules and dogmatic views. Ultimately, the nature of morality is too complex to be contained in a set of rules.[16]

It is for similar reasons that the Stoics didn't really go in for precepts. Like other Greek and Hellenistic philosophies, Stoicism embraced a form of virtue ethics, which means it was more concerned with character and the habits flowing from it than with following particular rules. The problem with rules, says Seneca, is that 'if we give precepts for specific situations, the task will be endless'. Instead, we should be guided by philosophical principles, which are 'concise and comprehensive'.[17]

For the Stoics, once we have really understood that a good life is one lived in accordance with our rational nature, that virtue is the only good and vice the only evil, and that everything else is indifferent, then we will be past the need for precepts. As Seneca explained, to a person who is already good, and so acts well, they are superfluous. But for someone who is not yet good, precepts are not enough because 'he ought to hear not only what is being prescribed to him but also why'.[18]

We can readily agree that it's impossible to give comprehensive guidance about particular situations, as there are too many contingent factors impinging on them. How to behave in a new relationship, for instance, will depend on a host of things like how the parties were affected by previous relationships, whether children are involved and so on.

Precepts can never cover every instance, and so always require interpretation. This is particularly the case in today's world, where there is little agreement about, for example, what counts as sexual misconduct or harm to sentient creatures. Rules are problematic, and ancient ones especially so.

Appropriate action

Apart from a little help from the precepts, how can we tell which actions might be consistent with the path and which it would be best to avoid? One discourse clearly defines actions in terms of their *consequences* on ourselves, other people and our future inclinations. Unwholesome action is any bodily, verbal or mental behaviour that 'has painful results', meaning that it 'leads to one's own affliction, or to the affliction of others, or to the affliction of both, and on account of which unwholesome states increase and wholesome states diminish'. Wholesome action, of course, is the opposite: it is bodily, verbal or mental behaviour that 'has pleasant results' and 'does not bring affliction'.[19]

But it's not just the actual actions we perform in the world that matter. Innovative among spiritual movements of the time, Buddhism gives most importance to *intention*, which is what determines karma and rebirth. The mental state that leads to unwholesome action is one tarnished by the defilements: greed, aversion and delusion.

This is further explained in the *Kālāma Sutta*, according to which it is the defilements that lead to harmful consequences. The greedy person, 'overcome by greed, with mind obsessed by it, destroys life, takes what is not given, transgresses with another's wife, and speaks falsehood; and he encourages others to do likewise', all of which leads to harm and suffering. The same goes for the aversive and the deluded person.[20]

We might think this is somewhat exaggerated: after all not all greedy people steal and kill. But it seems perfectly plausible that mental states like greed and aversion might cloud the mind to the point of bypassing reason's input and leading someone in their grip straight into impulsive and harmful actions.

In Stoicism, what counts as appropriate action is dictated mainly by an animal's nature.[21] In our case this means primarily acting in accordance with reason, but also includes the fact that we have a tendency to prefer certain things that are strictly speaking indifferent, such as being prosperous and in good health.

Intention also lies at the very centre of Stoic ideas, and it is what our actions stand or fall on. Seneca writes that the 'same acts may be either honorable or dishonorable: what counts is why or how they are done'. For instance, when 'a person sits by a sick friend, we approve. But doing this for the sake of an inheritance makes one a vulture awaiting a corpse.'[22]

Our position is likened to that of an archer: we intend to hit the target and do our best to do so, but actually hitting it is not a choice we can make. In the same way we can't control external circumstances or what happens in the world; all we can do is to 'aim right' and let go. Aiming right means acting with the intention of being a virtuous person and using reason to distinguish what matters from what doesn't. What actually happens once we have done our best should not be our concern. This is something worth remembering even if we're not Stoics, as it can remove much stress as we go about our daily business – preparing for exams or job interviews, staying healthy, trying to patch up a relationship.

Good emotions?

Knowledge of precepts and understanding appropriate action can help us to live ethically. But even more important is cultivating what could be called 'calm emotions'. For the Stoics, these were *joy*, *wishing* and *caution*. These are supposed to be a rational alternative to ordinary kinds of emotions: joy replaces pleasure, wishing replaces desire and caution replaces fear. But these are not, as one might think at first sight, just milder, more reasonable versions of their nefarious counterparts. Rather, they occur only in relation to virtue and/or lack of it, resulting in the limited emotional palette of joy at having acted virtuously, wishing that we were more virtuous, or caution when our virtue is in danger. No emotions other than the calm variety are considered legitimate.

There is another stumbling block: for the Stoics, only the sage is able to experience these calm emotions. That is why there is no rational equivalent of pain: this could only refer to lack of virtue, and we know that the sage cannot act less than virtuously. Unlike the rest of us, who can only have ordinary emotions (always fused with false views), the sage can have only good emotions.

In a way, these are not really emotions in our sense of the word. The difference between ordinary and Stoic joy, for instance, is vast. But there is no reason why, in our selective adoption of Stoic principles, we can't help ourselves to a more common-sense version of these as positive states of mind to cultivate, transforming unthinking lusts and panics into more manageable wishes and concerns. There are many things we might rightly value, such as harmonious relationships, being in nature, or getting over an illness. We could feel joy about these, wish to bring them about, and exercise caution about putting them at risk. As in REBT (p. 69), we could include a rational equivalent of pain – sadness, or disappointment – when such goods evade us.

Emotions like joy, wishing, caution and sadness can be appropriate responses to things so long as they are proportionate. We don't have to agree with the Stoic ideal of freeing ourselves from all emotion, but we can agree that we shouldn't get too joyful or distressed about things that are relatively unimportant. Emotions, as Aristotle advised, need to be moderated. But let's not kid ourselves that all unpleasant emotions can be replaced with milder ones: some situations in life call for full-blown pain.

Buddhism for its part offers us the so-called immeasurables, or divine abodes:

- goodwill/benevolence/kindness (*mettā*: this is usually translated as loving kindness)
- sympathetic joy (*muditā*)
- compassion (*karuṇā*)
- equanimity (*upekkhā*).

Like the Stoic ones, these are not best regarded as emotions. According to Bhante Bodhidhamma, they are attitudes, or 'ethical outcomes'.[23]

Mettā, for example, is not a feeling but refers to maintaining an attitude of friendliness and benevolence. It is the foundation of the other immeasurables, which is probably why it is the one most frequently mentioned in the early discourses. According to Anālayo, *mettā* is 'the water that nourishes the root' of the tree of compassion. It should permeate all our thoughts, actions and words, pervade all of our daily life.[24]

One discourse tells of the monk Anuruddha, who is living in harmony with two other monks, 'blending like milk and water'. He explains how he does it:

> 'I think thus: "It is a gain for me, it is a great gain for me, that I am living with such companions in the holy life." I maintain bodily acts of loving-kindness towards those venerable ones both openly and privately; I maintain verbal acts of loving-kindness towards them both

openly and privately; I maintain mental acts of loving-kindness towards them both openly and privately. I consider: "Why should I not set aside what I wish to do and do what these venerable ones wish to do?" Then I set aside what I wish to do and do what these venerable ones wish to do.'[25]

This spells out two important aspects of *mettā*: an appreciative attitude towards others and being prepared to let go of one's favoured ways of doing things.[26]

Mettā is the antidote required in situations in which anger, ill will and aversion have arisen, either in ourselves or others.[27] Anger is portrayed as an ugly condition: 'When an angry person is overcome and oppressed by anger, though he may be well bathed, well anointed, with trimmed hair and beard, dressed in white clothes, still, he is ugly.'[28] This chimes with Seneca's view that anger 'turns the fairest faces foul'.[29]

What we need at those times is *mettā*. It's not possible to have developed *mettā* and be in the grip of anger. A mind that has cultivated *mettā* is a beautiful mind.[30] *Mettā* is said to have several other, more pragmatic, benefits: better sleep; better relationships with human and non-human beings; reduced likelihood of being harmed by poison, weapons, water, fire or torture; and rebirth in a divine realm.

Just like *mettā* is the antidote for anger and ill will, sympathetic joy counters discontent, envy and jealousy. Similarly, compassion counters cruelty, and equanimity counters aversion.[31] Just as we can't have developed *mettā* and be angry, it's not possible to have developed the relevant immeasurable and still suffer from the parallel unwholesome state. The immeasurables complement each other, so it's important to cultivate all four.[32]

Compassion

Both Stoicism and Buddhism, then, see a place for 'calm emotions', even though in both traditions these are not emotions in the normal sense. Among these, compassion seems especially important for properly relating to others. Compassion literally means 'feeling with', but as we shall see, it doesn't have to refer to a feeling at all.

As we have seen (p. 110), in Stoicism compassion begins as a kind of self-concern and later extends to embrace fellow feeling. The Stoic philosopher Hierocles recommends an exercise for expanding the scope of our concern. He asks us to imagine that we are each surrounded by a series of concentric circles, spreading out from our own mind to our bodies, then to people with varying degrees of connection to us. Our task is to extend our concern from ourselves to our family, our neighbours, our community and ultimately the whole of humanity. Our true allegiance is to the community of rational beings: we are citizens of the universe.[33]

Different Stoic philosophers emphasise different parts of this doctrine. Seneca writes glowingly that:

> 'This universe that you see, containing the human and the divine, is a unity; we are the limbs of a mighty body. Nature brought us to birth as kin, since it generated us all from the same materials and for the same purposes, endowing us with affection for one another and making us companionable.'[34]

Epictetus sounds a less buoyant or inclusive note: not all human beings are rational or virtuous, and if they are not he advises not to 'consider them friends, any more than you can call them trustworthy, or constant, or brave, or free; no, do not even call them human beings, if you are wise'.[35]

For the Stoics, compassion is tricky, not the straightforwardly good thing one might expect. This is because it is based on a judgement that something bad has happened to someone. If we feel compassion for a beggar in the street, for instance, it can only be because we think they are in a bad situation. In Stoic terms this is an emotion, and like other emotions it betrays faulty views about the value of things indifferent. Just like in our own case it's not appropriate to feel pain as a result of things going wrong in the world, since these are in fact neither good nor bad, for the same reason it is equally inappropriate to suffer alongside another person. Epictetus advises not to think of a consul as a happy man, or a poor man as wretched: 'All these are judgements, and nothing more; and judgements concerning things outside our choice'.[36]

When we feel compassion, then, we are at least implicitly buying into an incorrect view of the world. If we 'feel with' someone who is distressed about being poor, for instance, we are de facto subscribing to their wrong beliefs. Stoics should know there is no reason to be upset in the first place. If we truly believed that virtue is the only good, why would we commiserate with those who suffer other kinds of losses? Compassion is therefore unfair both to the person who feels it and to the person on the receiving end of it, and not to be encouraged.[37]

But this doesn't mean an orthodox Stoic can have no compassion of any kind. It is open to the Stoic to acknowledge others' pain without buying into the faulty judgement that their situation is bad.[38] The important thing to remember is that what is bad is not the actual situation but the suffering person's understanding of it. It is a different kind of compassion: not an emotion, but a detached concern. As rational beings we have a responsibility to shift our mistaken judgement, and all we can really do for others is try to show them their own errors.

In Buddhism, compassion is clearly emphasised. It is the reason why the Buddha agreed to teach, and one of the four immeasurables. In the early texts, requests for teaching are often qualified with the expression 'out of compassion'.[39]

Compassion is the opposite of the intention to harm others. It is not defined precisely in the early literature, which often relies on stories to illustrate the concept. One of these is about a person on a long journey who becomes sick and exhausted. He is alone between two villages, both far away.[40] Someone comes along and, seeing this, reasons that if the sick traveller were to be accompanied to a village and given food and medicine he would definitely recover. In the same way, we should be concerned about other people being free from suffering, regardless of whether their actions are wholesome or unwholesome.

For Buddhism too compassion is not an undiluted blessing, however, as too much contemplation of suffering can lead to negative, aversive mental states. This lack of a neat separation between states can also be a problem for other immeasurables: *mettā*, for instance, can become confused with attachment. But there is a right way to be compassionate, and that is the Buddha's: just like him, we should practise compassion without attachment.[41] It is a bit like Aristotle's mean: we should aim to find the right balance between being unmoved by others' misfortunes and being overwhelmed by them.

Anālayo writes that cultivating compassion involves wishing others to be free from *dukkha*, which is different from dwelling on the suffering itself. Compassion is not best treated as 'suffering with' others, and need not and should not involve actual feelings of sadness.[42] It should be developed in conjunction with equanimity to counter any unwholesome effects.

The other danger of compassion is that it could lead to feelings of superiority, a habit of relating to others as though they were in a lesser position.[43] This, again, can be rebalanced by developing the other immeasurables, especially *mettā*, which involves goodwill towards everybody equally. Sympathetic joy also counteracts negative with positive, specifically encouraging us to feel pleased about other people's good fortune. Compassion, in the sense of wishing others to be free from suffering, should therefore be cultivated together with the other immeasurables and with insight into the nature of things.[44]

Compassion is a universal human virtue. We're all in the same boat, all fallible and ignorant human beings, all suffering in different but similar ways – surely giving and receiving compassion must be part of any good life. But, as we have seen, compassion can be understood in sometimes conflicting ways.

There are significant overlaps between compassion, empathy and sympathy, and the lines between these concepts are drawn in different places in different contexts. Various distinctions can be made, such as whether we are *sharing* other people's feelings or simply *understanding* them, and whether we are motivated to help. Nowadays it is empathy that tends to be seen as *the* crucial social quality, and often this is understood in the sense of sharing others' emotions.

But while it is certainly important to try to understand others' emotions, this 'feeling with' (whether we call it empathy or not) can be counterproductive and lead to burnout. Psychologist Paul Bloom warns that this kind of empathy tends to be biased and short-sighted, and can therefore easily lead us astray. One of his examples is that of people sending gifts and toys to a town where a high school massacre had occurred, with the consequence that hundreds of volunteers had to be recruited to store all the unrequired items into a big warehouse.

In place of empathy Bloom advocates compassion and concern, which 'don't require mirroring of others' feelings'.[45] This seems in tune with the forms of compassion advocated by Buddhism and Stoicism. In order to be compassionate we don't have to 'feel with' or necessarily share the value system of the person suffering. All we need is a sense of fellow feeling, a concern for others' well-being, and the wish to do what we can to relieve people's suffering. By not getting too caught up in the feelings of others, we can be more resilient and ultimately more helpful.

This is difficult to do in practice. To what extent should we expose ourselves to distressing news and situations, for instance? The answer depends partly on our existing habits and inclinations: if we have a tendency to close our eyes to others' suffering we can make an effort to open our heart a bit more; if we tend to get too involved and overwhelmed we can take a step back and remind ourselves that leaping in heart first can do more harm than good at times.

Modern psychology has identified another benefit of compassion. A growing body of research affirms its therapeutic importance, for oneself as well as others. Psychologist Paul Gilbert, originator of Compassion-Focused Therapy, explains that our difficulties in finding inner peace lie deep in our evolutionary past. We're still primarily motivated to protect ourselves from threats and to seek resources, and these two evolved systems are the sources of a lot of stress and anxiety. Fortunately, we have also evolved a soothing and affiliation system. Rooted in mammalian parental attachment, this generates a sense of calm and contentment.[46] All three systems are part of our repertoire, but Gilbert argues that in modern life they are out of balance. We can rebalance them, and counter threat-based emotions such as fear and anger, by developing our soothing and contentment system.[47]

Doing this requires practice. There are many exercises you could try. For instance, as you go about your daily life meeting people, you could remind yourself that each person is just like you, with qualities and flaws and joys and troubles, seeking to live as flourishing a life as possible. Or if you're feeling low or distressed, you could place your hand on your heart and say to yourself: 'This is a moment of suffering; suffering is part of everyone's life; may I be compassionate to myself in this moment.'[48]

Equanimity

Another attitude that is prominent in both Buddhism and Stoicism is equanimity. The Stoics used the term *apatheia* to refer to their ideal of being 'free from emotions' (which is what the term literally means), although different Stoics held different views on what exactly this involved. Both *apatheia* and *ataraxia*, or tranquillity, are close in meaning to *upekkhā* – the Pāli word for equanimity. (*Apatheia* is also the root of 'apathy', although the two terms have considerably different meanings.)

The Stoics took over the term *ataraxia* from Epicureanism, in which it meant freedom from anxiety. They also used it in that sense, but for them the focus was on imperturbability, which is less a mental state and more a character trait that 'renders the person that has it immune to influences that might interfere with his peace of mind'.[49] Stoic tranquillity is based on knowing that if one has virtue, one has all one needs. The Stoic sage has given up false beliefs about what is good, and is therefore free from agitation and emotionally unaffected by whatever fate brings.

In Buddhism, equanimity (*upekkhā*) is one of the four immeasurables, as described. It conveys the sense of looking upon the goings-on in the world with a balanced awareness.[50] Therefore it involves the ability to withstand the winds of fortune and avoid being upset by fluctuations in the eight worldly conditions of gain and loss, fame and disrepute, praise and blame, pleasure and pain (p. 96).

While goodwill, compassion and sympathetic joy are liable to turn into attachment or aversion, equanimity can counter these dangers through neutral observation, leaning towards neither pain nor pleasure, with the emphasis on allowing people to take responsibility for their own actions.[51]

But just as compassion needs equanimity to avoid sliding into a compulsive desire to help, equanimity could be corrupted by indifference and has to be tempered by compassion.[52] While equanimity is in some ways the culmination of the process of developing the immeasurables, it is not always superior, and there are times when the right thing to do is to intervene out of compassion, rather than remain a neutral observer. Cultivating equanimity is not meant to result in complete neutrality: the Buddha's example shows us that the ideal is some kind of 'unbiased concern'.[53]

Equanimity should therefore work in synergy with the other immeasurables and not undermine them. According to one discourse there are two types of equanimity, one to be cultivated and the other avoided. Just like with happiness, the criterion is whether the consequences are wholesome or unwholesome.[54]

Compassion and equanimity are complementary, and should be developed in tandem. But their marriage is a slightly awkward one: tranquil imperturbability and engaged compassion do not at first strike us as ideal bedfellows. In both traditions there is a tension between withdrawal and engagement, with the emphasis on detachment pulling more towards the former than the latter. For example, Nussbaum writes about the 'radical detachment of the Stoic sage, the detachment that greets slavery and even torture with equanimity, the detachment that receives the news of a child's death with the remarkable words, "I was already aware that I had begotten a mortal"'.[55]

One discourse celebrates detachment with the image of a rhinoceros:

> 'One whose mind is enmeshed in sympathy for friends and companions, neglects the true goal. Seeing this danger in intimacy, wander alone like a rhinoceros.

...

> As a deer in the wilds, unfettered, goes for forage
> wherever it wants: the wise person, valuing freedom,
> wanders alone like a rhinoceros.'[56]

It has been argued that compassion and equanimity are not inevitably in conflict. For a start, apparent callousness rooted in indifference could be simply a clear-headed assessment of reality. When Epictetus writes, 'if you kiss your child, or your wife, remind yourself that you are kissing a mortal; then you will be able to bear it if either of them dies', he is simply reminding us that it is in the nature of things that we are going to die and our spouses and children are going to die, and we had better get used to the idea.[57]

The Buddha had a parallel reminder:

> 'And what may be said to be subject to death? Wife
> and children are subject to death, men and women
> slaves, goats and sheep, fowl and pigs, elephants, cat-
> tle, horses, and mares are subject to death. ... One who
> is tied to these things ... being himself subject to death,
> seeks what is also subject to death.'[58]

Far from detachment and fellow feeling being in conflict with each other, Epictetus says, the former is actually essential for the latter. As we have seen, he argues that if we allow love to follow its normal course, personal interest can readily turn it to hate (p. 31), since 'every living creature is attached to nothing so strongly as to its own interest'.[59]

Also, we need to help ourselves before we can benefit

others: 'that one who is himself sinking in the mud should pull out another who is sinking in the mud is impossible; that one who is not himself sinking in the mud should pull out another who is sinking in the mud is possible', says the Buddha.[60]

Is it really possible to care with equanimity? Or is emotional turbulence the price we pay for caring? Does caring inevitably involve attachment? Philosopher Todd May thinks so. 'Caring,' he says, 'is a package deal. Either we care and expose ourselves to suffering, or we are serenely compassionate and do not.'[61] Perhaps rare people – sages – can attain a perfect balance, although we might reasonably doubt that this would be available to many, or that it would in any way resemble the sometimes messy, engaged love that fills our life with meaning. Perhaps, on the other hand, it is an impossible ideal.

The question is how far we should pursue detachment. First, we need to be wary of our motives. Wanting to avoid emotional upheaval is not a good rationale, as it could lead us to withdraw from potentially meaningful and enriching relationships and projects just for fear of pain. To the extent that we were successful in detaching, this might well take us away from, rather than closer to, living a good life. As Yalom writes, giving up important commitments to protect ourselves from being hurt would be 'like going on an ocean cruise and refusing to enter into friendships or interesting activities in order to avoid the pain of the inevitable end of the cruise'.[62]

Whatever our motives, detachment comes with costs as well as benefits. It may be that complete tranquillity, if it is possible, could be reached only by trading in some of our humanity, by making us more indifferent to what surrounds us than is good for us. Maybe full equanimity is neither achievable nor desirable for most of us. It is just our human make-up that the river of feelings keeps flowing whether we like it or not. And while it's good to be contented and untroubled, there are some things that as human beings we should be troubled about. A certain amount of upheaval may be the inevitable flip-side of caring.

Conclusion

Both the sage and the Buddha are somewhat high-minded role models that we can't hope to emulate directly. What we need to do is to seek incremental progress along a path of self-improvement. However, they can point us in helpful directions when trying to change ourselves for the better. They teach us that rules are not enough, and it is better to be inclined to do the right thing than reluctantly make ourselves follow precepts; that we need to check that we are acting on good intentions; that it's important to cultivate positive attitudes, making sure we deal with people kindly and thoughtfully, considering their interests and being motivated to help them.

The most distinctive intersection of Buddhist and Stoic ethics is the ideal of sympathetic detachment – a kind of engagement with others that comes from a place of non-attachment. This requires attaining an optimal blend of compassion and equanimity, combining appropriate engagement with the ability to avoid being tossed around by emotions.

This balance between compassion and non-attachment is an unstable one, and the traditions seem to tip towards detachment. But we can still take something from the ideal of equanimity. It makes sense to recalibrate our life in the direction of greater even-mindedness and tranquillity, since we normally tend to err very much in the opposite direction. According to May, it is not invulnerability that most people actually want, but 'a slightly less lacerating vulnerability'.[63]

Cultivating tranquillity is unlike chasing happiness. Running after an unreliable state like happiness is intrinsically unpredictable and ultimately unsatisfactory, while the ability to deal with life and emotions appropriately is the expression of a wisdom we've earned. But a tranquil state of mind does not trump all other concerns. Like compassion, equanimity should be developed with an eye on the Aristotelian mean: not too much, not too little.

Chapter 9

SPIRITUAL PRACTICE: BEYOND THEORY

Imagine you are interviewing for a chef. Whether the candidates can talk extensively about all the principles behind their cooking is unlikely to be the clincher: the decisive factor will be how good their food tastes.

Understanding is crucial, but it is not everything. This is certainly the case with Stoic and Buddhist theory. Appearances can be hard to resist. Our desires evolved over millennia and are not easily overcome, even when we see through them. Even if we know that certain things hold a false promise, we still suffer from a bizarre forgetfulness of what matters, obstinate in our determination to get worldly satisfaction. Appreciation of impermanence doesn't in itself stop us from perceiving the world as a glittering field of opportunities with the potential to make us happy ever after, if only we play our cards right. It is a challenge for these insights to make a real difference to how we feel and live.

In both Buddhism and Stoicism there is a keen awareness that while seeing things in the right light is essential, what matters most is putting what we have understood into practice. Far from being mainly an intellectual exercise, the path involves a deep transformation of all aspects of life. This doesn't come easily: it takes effort to shake off the daily habits and patterns that keep us heading in the wrong direction. This is where spiritual practice comes in. It is an indispensable part of the path, supporting and fostering moral and spiritual advancement.

In Buddhism, understanding is only one element of a path that also includes ethical foundations and meditative practice, as we have seen. It seems that early on the Buddha gave only sketchy instructions to his disciples about how to practise, which they were to some extent free to develop in their own way. Only later did these practices take a fixed form.[1]

The Hellenistic schools were fundamentally practical. For the Stoics, philosophy was not primarily about logic and argument but about the art of living. Epictetus, for instance, challenged the idea that we improve solely by reading books and acquiring knowledge. Instead, we should demonstrate that the knowledge has really sunk in: 'A builder does not come and say, "Listen to me talking on the art of building", ... but undertakes to build a house and proves by building it that he knows the art.'[2]

Like the builder who shows by building, our knowledge should shine through everything we do, Epictetus believes: eating, drinking, self-adornment, relationships, raising children, participating in the community. We should also show our understanding in the way we deal with others' abusive or inconsiderate behaviour.[3]

Taking our knowledge to heart and really living it, however, can be difficult, as Seneca illustrated with a literally colourful analogy:

'Just as some dyes are readily absorbed by the wool,
others only after repeated soaking and simmering, so
there are some studies that show up well in our minds
as soon as we have learned them; this one, though, must
permeate us thoroughly. It must soak in, giving not just
a tinge of color but a real deep dye, or it cannot deliver
on any of its promises.'[4]

Practical training, or spiritual practice (*askēsis*), was intended
to support philosophical understanding and embed it into
daily life. Students had to ensure that their newly acquired
values had taken root and the principles of the school were
consistently lived by. This required a vigilant outlook and a
daily discipline that would help them to overcome the habits
holding them back from the complete transformation of seeing and being they were seeking.

Our ability to make progress depends on identifying
the mechanisms by which self-improvement is possible and
developing the practices that can harness these. It's a bit like
trying to improve our health: we must first work out what is
necessary to reach that goal – losing body fat, building mus-
cle – then find practical ways to achieve it. The next section
looks at Buddhist and Stoic understandings of the mechanisms
of change.

Mechanisms of change

What are the main mechanisms that make change possible?
As humans, we can improve ourselves because we have the
ability to monitor our initial (faulty) responses to things
and then withdraw our (faulty) attributions of value and/or

challenge our (faulty) priorities. First we monitor, then we make changes.

In Buddhism, what we need to monitor is how contact with an object immediately produces a positive, negative or neutral 'feeling' (*vedanā*) – a basic reaction, which precedes anything we could call an emotion and is quickly followed by craving and clinging. Feelings constantly arise and cease in response to what we encounter.[5] Like the 'winds blow in the sky ... so too, various feelings arise in this body: pleasant feeling arises, painful feeling arises, neutral feeling arises.'[6]

Learning to catch these feelings as they appear is a really important part of the Buddhist training. Normally they tend to slip by, and as a result unwholesome states like greed and aversion quickly pile up. Before we know it there is a whole baroque structure – a 'mental proliferation' – of thoughts and emotions, and emotions about emotions, to contend with.[7]

It all starts with a simple moment, a primitive apprehension of something we are experiencing as good or bad, which we're not aware of unless we learn to pay attention to it. But even without properly entering our awareness this has the power to colour our thoughts and direct our actions. For instance, most of us have had the experience of meeting someone who 'presses the wrong button' for us, for reasons we don't understand. If we don't pick up on this ripple in our experience we might end up feeling suspicious and hostile, or otherwise acting out what the button has activated. But if we become more skilled at noticing that the button has been hit in the first place, we can cancel the activation. By training ourselves to spot the fluctuations of embryonic likes and dislikes as they come and go we can avoid being pushed around by them.

According to the Stoics too, we are constantly receiving 'impressions' about the state of the world and of ourselves in it. What these misleadingly tell us is that things outside our control are good or bad and we should pursue or avoid them. As they put it, we tend to automatically 'assent' to these impressions, which means that we believe them (this belief is implicated in emotion) and are likely to act on them.[8] But while animals and young children have no choice but to respond directly with action, adult human beings are in the fortunate position of being capable of suspending judgement if they have reason to think that the impression is not truthful.

The Stoics thought that we can and should learn to question and withdraw assent from such impressions. It can happen, however, that even a sage is momentarily affected by an appearance, without having assented to an incorrect impression. Given that we know the sage cannot experience bad emotions, this anomaly was explained through the idea of 'first movements': immediate, kind-of-physiological reactions that did not involve assent, so were not beliefs, or emotions, or connected with action.

This point was made through the story of a Stoic philosopher on a sea voyage, who during a violent storm showed every sign of being as frightened as everyone else. Does this mean he was assenting to the faulty judgement that something terrible was happening (that life is a good and losing it bad, for instance, which would be against Stoic philosophy)? It seems not. When the philosopher was subsequently asked how his reaction fitted in with his convictions, he explained, citing

Epictetus, that occasionally external impressions are too quick for us to withdraw our assent immediately.[9]

According to Seneca:

> 'Turning pale, shedding tears, the first stirrings of sexual arousal, a deep sigh, a suddenly sharpened glance, anything along these lines: whoever reckons them a clear token of passion and a sign of the mind's engagement is just mistaken and fails to understand that they're involuntary bodily movements.'[10]

In the Stoic scheme emotions are always under our control, as they require assent, and it is in our power to withdraw this. 'First movements' on the other hand are brief and beyond our control. We can learn to spot these and make sure they don't progress to actual emotions.

But even in ancient times this distinction was questioned: are these movements really not emotions? Of course, there are purely physiological reflexes, like blinking in the sun or producing tears when chopping onions, which involve no assessment at all. But Seneca's examples are not like this, and it seems reasonable to interpret both Stoic first movements and Buddhist feelings as expressing some kind of basic appraisal of how things are with the world and ourselves, some sense that something in the world is good or bad for us. Here it may be useful to go back to Nussbaum's neo-Stoic view that emotions are based on primitive appraisals, not necessarily on worked-out beliefs. This seems to be even more the case for these 'leanings', or proto-emotional responses.

These emotional hunches are highly fallible. Even if we

don't believe they are wrong most of the time, they mislead us at least some of the time, and so it would be useful to be more aware of them. We can't choose to eliminate them, but with training we can come to see that we don't need to believe them or act on them in a rush. This means first of all learning to catch them as they pop up. This is difficult, as by nature they often bypass conscious awareness. But if we practise monitoring our feelings we can become more sensitive to their subtle shifts. We can then move from being shunted into habitual patterns of reaction, based on unreflective values and impulses, to more reasoned and balanced responses.

Reasons to be optimistic?

For Buddhists and Stoics, self-improvement is possible through the mechanisms of change we have considered. The Stoics are optimistic about this, since while the body is only 'finely moulded clay', our faculty of reason is a portion of Zeus, as Epictetus puts it.[11] Quite unlike anything else in the world, our rational faculty is free, and this allows us to withdraw assent from the impressions constantly being produced through our contact with the world. We are fully in control of our thoughts and judgements, and therefore of our emotions.

As for Buddhism, although our behaviour is of course conditioned by the past, in the present moment we can still choose whether to respond to events with greed, hatred or delusion or their opposites – non-attachment, kindness and wisdom. This in turn will influence our future experiences and choices. But only a trained mind can do this.

Given what we've learned about the human mind and behaviour in recent years, however, we now know that we often overestimate the extent to which we are in control of our thoughts and actions. We have heard from psychologists and neuroscientists about how no more than a fraction of our mental processes may be conscious, the rest being insistently unconscious; about how limited our insight into our own thoughts and emotions is, how easy it is for us to make up stories about our motivations. Contrary to our assumptions, parts of us we never even glimpse may actually be in charge of much of what we do.

One of the best-known models in this respect is Daniel Kahneman's Systems 1 and 2. System 1 includes innate abilities that we share with other animals and all kinds of mental activities that have become automatic through practice: from basic abilities like object detection and perception of sounds to language understanding, reading social situations or driving a car. The main function of System 1, shaped by evolution, is to monitor and assess how an organism is faring in relation to challenges, threats or opportunities: 'Situations are constantly evaluated as good or bad, requiring escape or permitting approach.'[12] It is a blessing and a curse that this can never be switched off. System 2 on the other hand is conscious and deliberate, involving agency and choice. It requires putting attention and effort into complex mental activities: looking for someone in a crowd, doing your tax returns, performing complex calculations.

System 1 provides the raw data upon which System 2 builds. Impressions, intuitions and hunches become beliefs and voluntary actions. Most of the time, System 2 follows the suggestions of System 1 straightforwardly, without too much alteration: we believe our perceptions – it's hot – and act on our inclinations – we have a cold drink. Sometimes, however, the situation is more complicated, demanding more than automatic responses can deliver. In such cases, the conscious deliberation of System 2 comes to the fore, more actively suppressing or modifying the suggestions of System 1.[13] This can come in handy, for instance, in a social situation in which we have to act politely and contain feelings of anger towards a fellow guest.

System 1 does its work largely out of conscious sight, and this is resolutely going to stay that way. We can't make the unconscious conscious.[14] There is something we can do though, and that is to pay closer attention to our biases and distortions so that when they appear we are more able to counter them.[15]

Take implicit bias. We now know that stereotypes – about race or gender, for instance – can be held implicitly as well as explicitly; therefore we risk acting on them without even being aware they're there. For example, studies have shown that if the gender-identifying information of candidates is removed from their CVs, more women are invited for job interviews. Once we become aware of these unconscious prejudices, we can begin to take steps to counter them. If we're on an interview panel, for instance, we can at least ask ourselves some searching questions about our assessment of the interviewees: am I giving candidates equal attention? Is my mental image of the ideal candidate gendered?

Studies show that we suffer from many other distortions, for instance the tendency to think that we, and our children, are of above average ability. What Buddhism and Stoicism want us to free ourselves from are not just such obvious distortions, but our basic assessments of things being good or bad. Catching our everyday biases is difficult enough. Escaping from the deeper illusions is a much harder task, and requires a lifetime of training.

The training

As we have seen, both Buddhism and Stoicism made extensive use of practical training, and this often involved some form of meditation, in the broad sense of the word (p. 85).

Much has been lost about early Stoic practices, and we rely for information on the work of the later Stoics. Hadot writes that, unlike Buddhist meditation, 'Greco-Roman philosophical meditation is not linked to a corporeal attitude but is a purely rational, imaginative, or intuitive exercise that can take extremely varied forms.'[16] As far as we know, although the Stoics advocated performing certain daily practices, they did not have a formalised meditation programme. Their aim was to be aware of the principles of the school all the time and apply them to all aspects of life.

Unless we are frequently reminded of the correct way to think about things, it's easy to slip back into bad habits of thought, so Stoic meditation practice included for instance reading and memorising important philosophical principles. Doing this would help to internalise their wisdom, which would then always be available when required, like an ever-present personal coach. Seneca says:

'if we are situated in the midst of a noisy city, let there be a preceptor at our side to contradict those who laud vast incomes and to praise instead the man who is wealthy on little and who measures wealth by how it is used.'[17]

Stoic practice could also include what we might call visualisation exercises, such as imagining future tragedies (*premeditatio malorum*). The aim of these was to remind ourselves that such things are not evil, so that when the time comes we may respond with equanimity. 'The sea is calm now, but do not trust it: the storm comes in an instant. Pleasure boats that were out all morning are sunk before the day is over', writes Seneca.[18]

Another visualisation involves reflecting on the vastness of space and time, with the aim of recognising the insignificance of our problems. This form of practice was a favourite of Marcus Aurelius'. He writes that the mind can be cleared of junk by reflecting on the 'scale of the world' and on 'the narrow space between our birth and death; the infinite time before; the equally unbounded time that follows'.[19]

It is also important to set aside time, morning and evening, to examine ourselves and the way we are thinking and acting. This can help us to develop a clearer and more constant awareness of what does or does not depend on us, and so support our progress.

Some of the training involves putting the doctrines into practice. Musonius Rufus writes that the soul is strengthened by first reminding ourselves of the right perspectives and then moulding our actions to this understanding, so that we stop pursuing things that are not truly good and stop avoiding things that only *seem* bad. In this way, we 'won't welcome pleasure and avoid pain ... won't love living and fear death, and ... in the case of money, [we] won't honor receiving over giving.'[20]

In order to sustain our understanding and avoid wasting energy struggling with wayward motivation, we need to develop helpful habits. It is through repetition that new skills and qualities are built. Epictetus has this to say about the role of habits: 'Generally then, if you want to make something a habit, practise it; and if you do not want to make it a habit, do not do it, but get in the habit of doing something else. It is the same in relation to things of the mind.' This is important, because habits are fed by repeating certain actions. Whenever you give in to anger, for instance, you are actually strengthening the habit of behaving angrily.[21]

It takes effort to change habits. Yet change them we must, as we can move forward only if we disengage our attention from its habitual, automatic course and invest it in fresh new ways, supportive of a more correct vision of the world. This training is at the core of both Buddhism and Stoicism.

We can incorporate versions of this training in our daily lives. If we become aware that certain habits have consequences we don't want, we can take action to change them. For example, if our habitual checking of social media is starting to interfere with our real-world relationships, we can resolve to check no more than once or twice a day. If we are tempted to break our resolve, we can remind ourselves that the urge will pass, and that it is likely to become less frequent or intense over time. Similarly, if there are behaviours we would like to encourage, we can make concrete plans to do them regularly until they become second nature. If we think we need to become better listeners, we can make a conscious effort to give people our full attention, making sure we don't interrupt them or multi-task while they are talking.

Mindfulness and meditation

The ancients knew that experience is mediated by attention. One discourse says that whatever a monk 'frequently thinks and ponders upon, that will become the inclination of his mind'.[22] On a very similar note, Marcus Aurelius writes: 'The things you think about determine the quality of your mind. Your soul takes on the colour of your thoughts.'[23]

In normal circumstances we attend mostly to pleasure and pain, and we unquestioningly accept their dominance. According to philosopher Jeremy Bentham: 'Nature has placed mankind under the governance of two sovereign masters, pain and pleasure. It is for them alone to point out what we ought to do, as well as to determine what we shall do.'[24]

Buddhism and Stoicism instead suggest we need to train ourselves to become less reactive to the stimuli around us, more aware of our leanings towards pleasure and away from pain. For that we need *mindfulness* (*sati* in Pāli). A lot has been said and written about it of late, in the wake of the success of various health and mental health programmes based on mindfulness techniques. In these, mindfulness is generally defined as something like paying close attention to present-moment experience in a spirit of acceptance.

The word *sati* is used in different ways in the Pāli texts and does not map exactly on to the contemporary use of 'mindfulness'. In some ways it diverges from the modern usage of awareness of the present moment, veering more towards memory, recollection and a sense of keeping in mind the practice to be done. But the two meanings can be connected, since it is attention to the present moment that helps to take things in and remember them later.[25]

Mindfulness, then, can be seen as a way of paying attention.[26] Its primary function is that of observation and monitoring. The early texts evoke its meaning through a number of colourful similes: it is like a cowherd watching his cows from the distance, for instance.[27] Rupert Gethin explains that 'mindfulness seems always to be understood as a holding of attention on something; in some practices this involves holding the attention on the breath or the emotion of friendliness; in others, the emphasis is on holding attention on the way the mind works, that is, on the process of attention itself.'[28]

Mindfulness is an attitude or skill that can be developed in different ways. It can even blossom naturally from our character. Meditation is one way to cultivate it. As we have seen, meditation can refer to mental training of various kinds. In Buddhism, however, mindfulness is primarily associated with insight meditation (p. 46). The main text on this is the *Satipaṭṭhāna Sutta*, which gives instructions for establishing mindfulness through a close examination of various objects, including the body, feelings (pleasant, unpleasant or neutral) and wholesome or unwholesome mental states. Through this mindful investigation, the practices aim at insight into the impermanent nature of experience.

In Stoicism, likewise, if we want to make progress we need to cultivate attention (*prosochē*). As in Buddhism, training our attention is what makes it possible to be vigilant about our inner life, aware of our experience at a sufficiently fine-grained level to enable us to detect the initial stirrings of emotions, desires and aversions, and so avoid being carried away by them.

Psychologist Guy Claxton offers some fresh metaphors for this process of increasing awareness. If you speed up a film of a growing fern, he writes, you will lose sight of the actual process, and instead see a jump from no fern to fully grown fern. Likewise with our thoughts and feelings: they may seem to spring up fully formed from the depths, but in fact they must go through some process of 'unfurling'. Although the first 'seed' may be forever hidden to us, earlier stages of unfurling, including sensations, perceptions, thoughts and memories, may lie on the edge of consciousness and become accessible to us if we train our attention. By developing this kind of awareness, says Claxton, one 'is able to observe the shenanigans of one's own mind without either "attachment" or "aversion" ... Instead one can be just interested, amazed, and often amused by its firework display.'[29]

Observing mental states without reacting will slowly drain power from them, and in this way mindfulness can 'de-automatise' habitual responses.[30] This does not come easily: after all, as we've seen, there are good evolutionary reasons why we are constantly reacting positively or negatively to all sorts of things. In a way, non-reactivity and equanimity go against the grain of human nature. Hence the need for practice.

But why would we put in the effort in the first place? The traditional purpose that is most relevant for us today is ethical. If we want to improve ourselves and live a good life we need to find ways of dealing with unwholesome states and developing wholesome ones. Mindfulness is an exceptionally useful tool for that.

It is unclear, however, to what extent mindfulness can lead to more wholesome states on its own. We can easily conceive of attention skills being put to bad uses, if untethered from ethical training. Different Buddhist schools have taken different positions on this. According to one point of view, a more ethical outlook arises naturally from the practice, so it's not possible to perform an unwholesome action while being mindful: by creating a certain distance from states like greed and aversion, mindfulness should stop us acting on them. But in the main, the early Buddhist texts make it clear that there is a right and a wrong mindfulness, with the right kind occurring in close relationship with other elements of the eightfold path.[31]

To use mindfulness in the service of living ethically, we need it to 'guard the doors of our sense faculties', to monitor the senses in order to avoid being overwhelmed by desire, much like the gatekeeper of a town who 'allows entry to the good and keeps out the bad'.[32] What happens if such restraint is not established is illustrated in a discourse that tells the story of a monk who 'goes into a village or town for alms with his body unguarded, with his speech unguarded, with mindfulness unestablished, and with sense faculties unrestrained. He sees a woman there lightly clothed, lightly dressed. When he sees such a woman, lust infects his mind', as a result of which he abandons his Buddhist training.[33] Like lust, other unwholesome states easily enter our minds when mindfulness is lacking.

Epictetus' writings are in tune with this approach, but he strikes a more martial note when he says that the philosopher 'keeps watch over himself as over an enemy in ambush'.[34] For him, 'we should be satisfied if, by never relaxing our attention, we shall escape at least a few errors.'[35] Seneca writes in similar tones about anger being an enemy that 'must be held at bay on the first frontier; when it has entered and made its way through the gates, it accepts no limits from those it has taken captive.'[36]

Secular mindfulness programmes have drawn on the techniques described in the *Satipaṭṭhāna Sutta* for different purposes: not for ethical, spiritual or existential reasons but for the relief of pain or distress, or increased well-being. Arguably, however, such outcomes hinge on exactly the same mechanisms.

Research in this area has been mushrooming and seems to be yielding good results for mindfulness and meditation for all kinds of life issues and conditions – mental health, pain management, even the enhancement of cognitive abilities as we age. One could get the impression that mindfulness can solve any problem. But before we buy into a 'magic wand' outlook we should be aware that the research is beset by methodological flaws, only some of which are: the lack of an agreed definition of mindfulness; the unevenness of the studies, with some focusing on patients in clinical environments and others on long-term committed practitioners of a spiritual path; and the fact that interventions tend to be multi-component and it's hard to tease apart which are doing what work. The clinical evidence is positive but mixed.

One concern with secular mindfulness is that it can be used to sustain rather than challenge a materialistic lifestyle. We can, however, mitigate this if we approach mindfulness in the right spirit. Far from being the royal road to hot sex or making your million, the proper use of mindfulness involves nipping in the bud the false impressions and pleasant or unpleasant feelings that set unwholesome states into motion. The more we practise, the more we move away from the mindless reactivity into which our particular collections of habits and compulsions propel us, and towards reflectivity and autonomy. We may lack the freedom to transform ourselves completely, but there is some scope for a limited makeover.

Simply keeping a mindful attitude may or may not prevent or dissipate unwholesome states. What if it doesn't? Epictetus comes up with an excellent tip. We should monitor our impressions of pleasure and pain, then think through the consequences of acting on them, and on that basis decide how to respond:

> 'If you are dazzled by the appearance of a promised pleasure, guard yourself against being carried away by it; but let the matter wait, and allow yourself some delay. Then bring to mind both points of time: that in which you will enjoy the pleasure, and that in which you will repent and reproach yourself after you have enjoyed it; and set before you, in opposition to these, how you will rejoice and praise yourself if you abstain.'[37]

The *Vitakkasaṇṭhāna Sutta* also has some good advice. In ascending order of difficulty, we should:

- reflect on something more wholesome
- think about the consequences of the unwholesome thoughts

- remove attention from the unwholesome thoughts
- remove the source of the unwholesome thoughts.

Only in the very last resort, the Buddha says in untypically truculent language, should we 'with clenched teeth and the tongue pressing on the palate, restrain, subdue and beat down the (evil) mind by the (good) mind'.[38]

Generally, if plagued by troublesome thoughts, we can either chase them with other thoughts, or take a more detached attitude towards them. In this respect, the two traditions have a different focus, as in Stoicism faulty beliefs should be confronted and replaced with truthful ones, whereas detached observation is the more common Buddhist approach. The potential danger of fighting thoughts with thoughts is that of becoming even more entangled in rumination. But ultimately, both approaches aim at a similar mental shift.

The way of detachment is also the approach of Acceptance and Commitment Therapy (ACT). In ACT, being human inevitably means experiencing a constant stream of thoughts and feelings, some of them uncomfortable. This is not a problem in itself, but it becomes one when we identify or fight with these, as we tend to do. The key to psychological flexibility, in ACT, is to allow experience to unfold in the knowledge that thoughts and feelings come and go. The goal is not removing or promoting any particular mental state: it is to be able to live a rich life regardless of how we may be feeling at any particular time.[39]

This is explained through similes and practical exercises. In the 'passengers on the bus' metaphor, for instance, thoughts are compared to a bunch of critical and abusive passengers on a bus you're driving. You're in charge of the bus, though, so you can let the passengers shout as much as they like: that doesn't stop you heading towards your valued destination.

The important shift, it seems, is to a more 'decentered' attitude, which means that we are able to observe our experience instead of being completely fused with it. It has been suggested that underpinning such a shift may be three inter-related cognitive processes:

- *Meta-awareness* refers to being aware of one's experience as a process: not only being angry but being aware that you're angry, almost as if looking at yourself from the outside.
- *Disidentification* from one's experience involves experiencing thoughts and emotions as separate from yourself: you're aware that you are angry and see it as a passing state, not part of you.
- *Reduced reactivity* to thought content means that having a thought doesn't immediately lead to a build-up of more thoughts, emotions and motivations to act: an angry thought does not necessarily entail more angry thoughts or angry actions.

These processes have been linked with mental health.[40] As mentioned before, however, they seem to be the very same ones that can facilitate personal and ethical development.

Psychologist Rollo May was in tune with Buddhist and Stoic thinkers when he said that: 'Human freedom involves our capacity to pause between the stimulus and response and, in that pause, to choose the one response toward which we wish to throw our weight.'[41]

Death and body meditations

If secular mindfulness exercises are familiar and comforting, some of the practices described in the *Satipaṭṭhāna Sutta*
are more disturbing. These confirm that mindfulness is
not always present-centred, as per the modern definitions.
Meditations on death and on body parts, for instance, make
more use of memory and the imagination. Nor is it always
non-judgemental, writes Rupert Gethin, as 'the meditator is
directed not just to observe the body parts, but to hold them
in mind as "impurities"'.[42]

Both Stoicism and Buddhism use vivid imagery about
death and decay with the clear rationale of challenging our
flawed perceptions of reality and stopping in its tracks our
inclination to see value where there is no value. They are
meant to help us to keep in mind that the things we are constantly wanting are neither valuable nor lasting.

As we have seen, these false views of the world are not
harmless; they are at the root of our frustrating experience
of life. We may understand this intellectually, but something
more engaging is required to cut through ordinary appearances. That's what these hard-hitting kinds of mental training
are designed to do.

One of Marcus' preferred methods is to redefine things we
covet but that don't depend on us so as to bring to the fore the
rot and decay that are always at work behind the deceptively
shiny surfaces: 'At all times, look at the thing itself – the thing
behind the appearance – and unpack it by analysis'.[43]

In this way we will be reminded of their true nature
and come to a more 'objective' judgement. It is, Marcus says,
like:

'seeing roasted meat and other dishes in front of you and suddenly realizing: This is a dead fish. A dead bird. A dead pig. Or that this noble vintage is grape juice, and the purple robes are sheep wool dyed with shellfish blood. Or making love – something rubbing against your penis, a brief seizure and a little cloudy liquid.'

Flesh is a 'mess of blood, pieces of bone, a woven tangle of nerves, veins, arteries.' Human lives are 'yesterday a blob of semen; tomorrow embalming fluid, ash.'[44]

In Buddhism, there are many similar reminders of the unattractive and impermanent nature of the body. A whole section of the *Satipaṭṭhāna Sutta* is devoted to body meditation. This starts with awareness of breathing, then moves on to posture, bodily activities, anatomical parts, the four elements (earth, water, air, fire) and corpse in decay. Some of these, in particular anatomical parts and corpse in decay, seem very in tune with Stoic perspectives.

The contemplation of anatomical parts, for instance, is about paying attention to what we're made of. We should mentally break down the body into its constituent parts, examining it 'from the soles of the feet and down from the top of the hair, enclosed by skin and full of many kinds of impurity':

'head hairs, body hairs, nails, teeth, skin, flesh, sinews, bones, bone marrow, kidneys, heart, liver, diaphragm, spleen, lungs, bowels, mesentery, contents of the stomach, faeces, bile, phlegm, pus, blood, sweat, fat, tears, grease, spittle, snot, oil of the joints, and urine.'[45]

This is not meant to provoke aversion, but equanimity. It is like:

> '... a man with good eyes who has opened a double-mouthed bag full of different sorts of grain, such as hill rice, red rice, beans, peas, millet, and white rice, which he would examine: "This is hill rice, this is red rice, these are beans, these are peas, this is millet, and this is white rice."'

This is quite challenging. But even more demanding is the meditation on corpses. In ancient India corpses were left out in 'charnel grounds', and people would have had the opportunity to observe the various stages of decomposition. The text describes these in some detail, from 'a corpse thrown aside in a charnel ground – one, two, or three days dead, bloated, livid, and oozing matter ... being devoured by crows, hawks, vultures, dogs, jackals, or various kinds of worms' to 'bones bleached white, the colour of shells ... bones heaped up, more than a year old ... bones rotten and crumbling to dust'. The monk reminds himself that 'this body too is of the same nature, it will be like that, it is not exempt from that fate.'[46]

By focusing our attention on decay, these practices bring home the fact that the body, which we might normally perceive as attractive and desirable, is actually no such thing. By keeping the awareness of impermanence and death at the front of our minds, they aim to counter sensual desire and ultimately reach a certain detachment. Death will not deprive us of anything important.

Of course, some of these lessons are worth remembering: even if we have a great life, it will eventually come to an end, and so will the lives of the people we love. But there are a couple of points to consider. The practices are supposed to lead to some kind of equanimity – as exemplified by the simile of the bag of grains and beans – not to loathing and aversion. But they could conceivably have the opposite effect and make us depressed. In an age when body dysmorphia and eating disorders are all too common, it is important to avoid drawing the wrong lessons.

The Buddha does warn that if such a practice were to elicit loathing, the monk should switch to a different one. A discourse reports the case of a group of monks who engage so enthusiastically with contemplating the unattractiveness of the body that a number of them end up committing suicide. On finding out what happened, the Buddha decides to teach the survivors mindfulness of breathing instead.[47]

In theory, these meditations could help us to appreciate the present moment more. On the other hand, they might make us too death-focused to appreciate anything. It's a bit like putting on a fur coat in summer because we'll need it at Christmas, wrote Montaigne, who was aware of the danger: 'It is certain that most preparations for death have caused more torment than undergoing it.'[48] We need to be aware of that risk too.

Some of these practices may well help some of us to maintain a wise perspective on life. But most of the time for most people it may be enough to stick to gentler reminders of impermanence rather than really go for the gory details. Reminding ourselves that we will die may be enough.

Seneca has a wealth of such reminders: 'Everything is dangerous and deceptive and more changeable than the weather; everything tumbles about and passes at fortune's behest into its opposite; and in all this tumult of human affairs there is nothing we can be sure of except death alone.' Since there is 'no way to know the point where death lies waiting for you, ... you must wait for death at every point'.[49]

Anālayo recommends bringing mortality into one's present-moment awareness through a breathing meditation: 'with every breath coming in one is aware that this could be one's last inhalation, and with every exhalation one trains oneself to let go and relax.' He suggests that if we are feeling agitated, we should put more emphasis on the exhalation; if sluggish, on the inhalation. 'Every breath,' he writes, 'closer to death'.[50]

Conclusion

Dazzled by the possibility of self-improvement, we shouldn't lose sight of our vulnerability and limitations. We are largely the result of things we have no control over, such as genes and upbringing, and our access to unconscious processes is limited or non-existent, no matter how much we 'look inside'. This of course doesn't mean giving up on trying to improve, only that we have to be realistic about what is possible and bear in mind that perfection can only be a distant ideal.

If we are content with more modest goals there is a lot we can do through instruction and training, effort and attention. One thing we can do is learn to become more accepting of mortality. In the modern world, death is so often kept out of sight, concealing even the connection between a living animal and a piece of meat. Perhaps that is why ancient forms of death meditation seem so macabre today. That is all the more reason why some version of them is needed now.

Much of what we can do hinges upon developing mindfulness to catch the first stirrings of emotions, engrained habits and patterns of reaction. Setting aside time for meditation is one way to do it. Another way is weaving into our daily life what we could call 'micro-meditations', in which we stop for a moment and check in with ourselves: how am I *really* feeling? How am I responding to things? Even without any formal exercises, we can learn to become more aware of our automatic responses.

We may never be completely transparent to ourselves but there is a clear difference between self-awareness and self-delusion, and with practice we can get better at distinguishing them. By becoming more aware of things we otherwise don't pay much attention to, we can learn to better control how we respond to them. This is what wisdom is all about, and what spiritual traditions help us to achieve.

Chapter 10

MEDITATIONS
FOR A BETTER LIFE

Change is difficult. That's why both traditions see the need for a practice: a set of exercises to be performed with disciplined regularity. We too could benefit from developing our own practice, building working on ourselves into our daily routines.

The following ten meditations are inspired by Buddhist and Stoic insights and aim to put some of them into action. They deal with *acceptance*, *awareness* and *attention*: becoming more accepting of impermanence, more aware of ourselves and more attentive to what we value in life.

1. Get the self-monitoring habit

To catch the first signs of unhealthy desires, or potentially destructive emotions, like fear or anger, we have to start by paying attention to our immediate reactions to things. Seneca puts it well: 'Just as signs of a rainstorm arrive before the storm itself, so there are certain signs that announce the coming of anger, love, and all those storm gusts that vex our minds.'[1]

An important practice in this respect is mindfulness of feelings (*vedanā*), which involves learning to catch early reactions towards or away from the stimuli we encounter in our daily life. Doing this will give us the chance to question those feelings and ask ourselves what really matters before we are too deeply mired in unwholesome reactions.

Formal meditation can help with this, but with some attention we can all get better at catching those first stirrings. The Stoics advised thinking ahead to the challenges of the day in the morning and reviewing the day just gone in the evening, in an effort to identify where we can improve. Epictetus says: 'as soon as you are up in the morning, consider what you need in order to enjoy tranquillity. Ask yourself: "In what do I consist? Merely in body, in estate, in reputation? None of these. What, then? I am a rational creature. What, then, is required of me?" [In the evening], reflect on your actions: ... What did I do that was unfriendly or unsociable? What did I fail to do that I should have done?'[2]

In the same spirit, you could set aside a few minutes in the morning to remind yourself of the values you'd like to guide your day, and in the evening to review what went well and what needs to be improved. This kind of self-monitoring can also be done informally throughout the day, simply getting into the habit of questioning your reactions to things.

Another useful way to reflect on our reactions is what in Buddhist texts are known as 'four great efforts':

- preventing unwholesome states from arising in the first place;
- letting go of unwholesome states that have already arisen;
- promoting wholesome states;
- maintaining wholesome states.[3]

Similarly, Seneca writes that 'the first goal is not to become angry, the second is to cease when angered, and the third is to cure another's anger too'.[4]

It's not always easy to prevent unwholesome states from arising. Perhaps it's a little easier to learn to become aware of these quickly and take remedial action, such as encouraging a more wholesome state. If anger or envy arise, for instance, you could aim to be mindful of this, remind yourself it's not a state you want to dwell in, and see if you can gently nudge yourself to adopt a more kindly or generous attitude.

It might also be beneficial each day to take regular pauses for a few minutes of what one could call 'calm abiding'. This is the time, Bhante Bodhidhamma suggests, to check in with ourselves and interrogate our intention. If it's wholesome we should encourage it; if unwholesome, allow it to pass.

2. Question your thinking

One of the most quoted Stoic sayings must surely be Epictetus' (which we first encountered on p. 39): 'People are disturbed not by things, but by the views they take of things.'[5]

It is certainly good advice to examine our thinking about all kinds of things. We should indeed question our views and interpretations of events. It would be helpful to get into the habit of asking ourselves questions like: am I right to think this? What is my evidence for it? Are there better alternative explanations? Should I suspend judgement on this one?

But the particular kind of questioning Epictetus had in mind was about whether things are in our power or not. If not, we should drop our concern for them. We've seen why it's more complicated than that. First of all there is no neat division between what we can and what we can't control. Rather there is a spectrum, from things we can't control at all to those over which we have *some* influence. But the spectrum stops here, as there is nothing over which we have complete control.

At one end of the spectrum, indisputably we have no control over the past, although it is amazing how many hours we are able to spend replaying in our head some situation that we wish had turned out differently, almost as if by doing that the outcome might actually change. Equally indisputably, we are powerless over our ultimate date with death.

At the other end is the sphere of choice. We now know it's not the case that this is wholly in our power, as Epictetus believed. Nonetheless, there is some scope for changing our views and attitudes, although in view of the large unconscious input the difficulty of the task should not be underestimated.

Most things fall within a grey area. We have a certain amount of control over the course of our life. We can do things that are likely to be beneficial for our health, for instance, although we should combat the wishful thinking that if we go to the gym and adopt the right diet we can stave off all illnesses and live well into our hundreds. We can increase our chances of getting a job if we make sure we prepare for the interview. But can we change other people? Can we change our talents and inclinations? The answer is probably either not at all or only to a very limited degree, depending on the circumstances and how we go about it.

Once we have done all we can, in relation to our health, a job, or anything else, we should accept that outcomes in the world are due to many different factors that are not up to us, and let go of our fantasies of control. We may get ill despite our healthy diet and exercise, and we may not get the job even though we're well-qualified and prepared. For this reason we should avoid making our well-being entirely dependent on things turning out as we'd prefer. If something is very import- ant we may want to leave no stone unturned. But if it looks like things are just not going to work out, we should accept it, because the bottom line is we can't do anything about it. There is a fine line between trying our best and not only wasting time but also tormenting ourselves and others fighting against things that can't be changed.

A modified version of Chrysippus' questions might be use- ful. He asked: 'Is there good or bad at hand? Is it appropriate to react?' This could be supplemented with a few more, produc- ing a kind of Chrysippan flowchart:

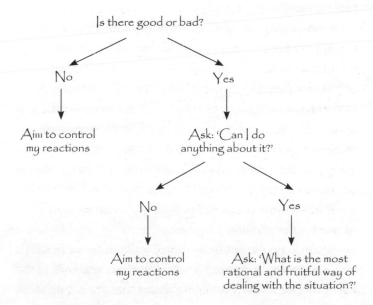

Is there good or bad?

No → Aim to control my reactions

Yes → Ask: 'Can I do anything about it?'

No → Aim to control my reactions

Yes → Ask: 'What is the most rational and fruitful way of dealing with the situation?'

3. Remind yourself that 'it's a cup'
According to Epictetus' classic advice:

> 'With regard to any object that either delights the mind, or is useful, or is fondly loved, remind yourself of its nature, beginning with the merest trifles. If you have a favourite cup, [remind yourself] that it is a cup you are fond of; then, if it is broken, you won't be upset'.[6]

As we have seen, Epictetus goes on to say we should apply this to human relationships, so that even the death of loved ones does not perturb us. For many of us, this will seem excessive. Although we should acknowledge and accept that we and the people we love will die, we might prefer to use this method primarily in relation to cups – or cars, rugs, leaking roofs, or jobs. It's fine and good to cultivate a relative indifference towards possessions, but applying this to people is more problematic. Generally, our goal should be to give things their *right* value.

As Epictetus suggests, however, we should question excessive attachment to wealth and possessions, because material things will not give us lasting well-being, and concentrating on obtaining and keeping them can divert us from more worthwhile pursuits. Excess and accumulation are based on the wrong values and are a distraction from what really matters.

If we reflect on it, we will probably find that much of what we own is not genuinely valuable. Nor do we need to spend money on luxury goods when more modest ones work just as well. As Seneca points out, 'Whether that house is built of sod or of variegated marble from foreign lands is of no significance:

believe me, a person can be sheltered just as well with thatch as with gold.'[7] (Although this hits a slightly false note, coming as it does from a man of fabulous wealth.)

The advice to simplify our lives brings to mind William Morris' dictum that we should have nothing in our houses that we don't know to be useful or believe to be beautiful. More recently, Marie Kondo has suggested that unless an object 'sparks joy' in our heart, we should get rid of it. It's easy to see the appeal of these rules of thumb: many of us feel a bit oppressed by the stuff we accumulate, and there's a certain sense of liberation in shedding some or even much of it.

Although this approach has benefits, the advice we can take from Buddhists and Stoics goes further. True, radically pruning our desires and nurturing a mindful appreciation of what we have can also bring tranquillity and contentment. But the simplicity of the ancient traditions is more about orientating ourselves to what is truly of value in life than it is about aesthetics, life management or feeling good.

4. Don't get hung up on status and reputation
These things are generally not a reliable measure of worth. Aristotle's advice may help us here: recognition matters only when we're being recognised by people we respect and for good reasons. These are good criteria, and we could do with checking more often whether they apply.

As for not being recognised, we are all complex individuals with qualities and flaws, and the virtues we happen to have are not necessarily the most celebrated in our culture. Kindness, generosity or curiosity, for instance, are often overlooked in favour of things like beauty, wealth or power.

Marcus Aurelius puts his finger on it when he says:

'It's quite possible to be a good man without anyone realizing it. Remember that. And this too: you don't need much to live happily. And just because you've abandoned your hopes of becoming a great thinker or scientist, don't give up on attaining freedom, achieving humility, serving others'.[8]

Contrary to the traditional value of modesty, nowadays we are often encouraged to advertise our talents and achievements to the world. But the philosophers' advice is that it's better not to blow our own trumpet. 'Your qualities should face inwards', says Seneca.[9]

If Aristotle's criteria apply, on the other hand, and we're being recognised by people whose values we share and for good reasons, we might feel entitled to a certain amount of pride. Not too much though: it is through accidents of birth and other chance factors that we acquired many of our qualities and talents. Moreover, vanity and conceit can be sneaky and we need to guard against them.

Generally, we should cultivate a healthy, balanced attitude regarding other people's opinion. It's true that we all have blind spots, and sometimes we need to hear what our friends have to say about our character and behaviour even if we don't like it. But we should not depend on external opinion too much. Epictetus says:

'If anyone tells you that such a person speaks ill of you, do not make excuses about what is said of you, but

answer: "He was ignorant of my other faults, otherwise
he would not have mentioned only these.'"[10]

Four of the Buddha's eight worldly conditions, about which
we should cultivate equanimity, are fame and disrepute, praise
and blame. The Buddha advised the monks to be neither too
pleased when people praised him nor too upset when they
spoke disparagingly of him, since this would only be a hin-
drance on their path.[11] Instead, they should calmly correct or
confirm what has been said.

Finally, we should remember that climbing up career lad-
ders for the sake of status and reputation has a cost. Seneca
expresses it well:

'So, when you see a man repeatedly taking up the
robe of office, or a name well known in public, don't
envy him: those trappings are bought at the cost of
life.'[12]

This is why those who value their work above all else often
end up feeling they have no life left to themselves. Success
can come at the price of time to think and reflect, to enjoy
the company of others, or simply to appreciate the small joys
of everyday life.

5. Radiate goodwill

We have to be realistic: human relationships can be difficult;
people often behave badly and let us down. In order to deal
with this fact as wisely as possible, it's best to be prepared.
Marcus Aurelius writes:

> 'When you wake up in the morning, tell yourself: The
> people I deal with today will be meddling, ungrateful,
> arrogant, dishonest, jealous, and surly.'[13]

On the other hand, we're all flawed and imperfect beings, so
we should cut people some slack. 'The wise man will not be
angry with wrongdoers', says Seneca, because 'he knows that
very, very few turn out wise in the whole expanse of time.'[14]
When people act badly towards us, we should remember
that they usually have no idea that they are doing anything
wrong. We could say to ourselves: 'It seemed so to him',
as Epictetus puts it.[15] Thinking more generally about how
things seem to others allows us to see their points of view
better and to become more understanding. Marcus also
writes that:

> 'To feel affection for people even when they make mis-
> takes is uniquely human. You can do it, if you simply
> recognize: that they're human too, that they act out of
> ignorance ... and that you'll both be dead before long.
> And, above all, that they haven't really hurt you. They
> haven't diminished your ability to choose.'[16]

A basic stance of goodwill and compassion towards others
is a good place from which to face the world, rather than a
default position of irritable grumpiness. We all face the same
predicament, and compassion is the appropriate response. As
Hierocles advised (p. 121), we should practise extending our
fellow feeling outwards from ourselves, to our family, friends,
neighbours, community and the world.

One way of developing these qualities is through the meditative practice of radiating the relevant attitude in all directions. The simile used in the Buddhist texts is that of blowing a conch shell from a mountaintop so that the sound pervades the four directions.[17] We could sit quietly and evoke a sense of goodwill, or compassion, imagining that we are radiating it all around us, finally pervading the whole world.

6. Don't be too optimistic

All lives contain pain and heartache. Being human, Epictetus reminds us, entails:

> 'that you should at one time be sick; at another, take a voyage, and be exposed to danger; sometimes be in want; and possibly die before your time. Why, then, are you displeased? ... For it is impossible, in such a body, in such a world, and among such companions, that such things should not happen, some to one and some to another.'[18]

Over a lifetime, we can expect many things to go wrong, and we need to remind ourselves that this is normal. If we really accept this, we might be less put out when bad things happen, less inclined to feel hard done by, as if by our birthright they shouldn't befall us. This is how Seneca puts it:

> 'You were troubled by pain in your bladder, you received worrying letters, your losses continued – let me get to the point, you feared for your life. Well, didn't you know that in praying for old age, you were praying

for these things? A long life contains them all, just as a
long journey contains dust, mud, and rain.'[19]

The Stoics also advise imagining all kinds of possible disasters, as we have seen. What takes years to grow can be cut
down in seconds, says Seneca; empires can be overturned in
a moment. He recommends rehearsing in our minds the possibility of 'exile, torture, war, shipwreck'.[20] Seneca believes this
will help: 'You cannot escape these things', he writes, 'but you
can rise above them, and you will succeed in doing so if you
frequently reflect on and anticipate the future.'[21]

The question is whether imagining potential future disasters really is a good strategy to deal with them. Should we
be looking ahead to bankruptcy, divorce, illness or unemployment? There does seem to be something useful about getting
into such a habit. Thinking about these eventualities might
help us to prepare psychologically and possibly also practically.

But there is a danger of focusing on future evils so much
that we see nothing but gloom. When using any of these
reminders, therefore, we should check what effect they are
having on us. If we're getting depressed, it is probably because
we're thinking something like 'such and such a thing might
happen and it's the end of the world', as opposed to 'such and
such a thing might happen and if it does it's natural and I'll
deal with it as best I can'. It's the latter we need to encourage.

When planning for the future, it might be useful to follow
the Stoics' suggestion of adding to our intention a tag like 'if
nothing prevents' – a secular version of 'God willing' – as we
simply don't know whether the world will cooperate in making
our plans come to fruition. But we must take care not to take

this too far, or do it in a superstitious way, as if by anticipating bad things we can avert them.

An alternative point of view is that conjuring up bad things in our minds is a waste of time: we'll deal with them when they come. Even Seneca sometimes takes a more common-sense line, reminding us that the things we fear may never happen, or not be as bad as we anticipate.[22]

If we do adopt some form of anticipation of doom, we should make sure we counterbalance it with joyful thoughts and activities. An Epicurean technique, for instance, is to savour pleasant memories. If we manage this balancing act, the awareness that bad things are a normal part of life can heighten rather than obscure appreciation of what is good, just as a light stands out most clearly in the dark.

7. Think about death (but not too much)

Most of us avoid thinking about death as much as possible. To do so, however, is to refuse to face one of the most important facts of existence. The Buddha advises us to confront these head-on by reminding ourselves daily of the following truths:

'I am of the nature to grow old; I cannot avoid ageing.
I am of the nature to become ill; I cannot avoid illness.
I am of the nature to die; I cannot avoid death.
All that is mine, dear and delightful, will change and vanish.'

A fifth truth reminds us that actions have consequences.[23] On the death of one of his chief disciples, the Buddha tells his attendant Ānanda not to be sad or distressed: 'What arises, what occurs, what is constructed, is of a nature to be destroyed. How could it not be destroyed? Wishing for it not to be destroyed is [wishing] for what is impossible.'[24]

For the Stoics, the practice of remembering that we and those we love will die is really an application of the more general one of highlighting that external things are vulnerable and disasters around the corner. Epictetus advises us to remind ourselves that what we love is mortal. It is like 'a fig, or a bunch of grapes, [available] in the appointed season. If you long for these in winter you are a fool. So, if you long for your son, or your friend, when you cannot have him, remember that you are wishing for figs in winter.'[25]

But we should not demand too much of ourselves. Even Seneca did not toe the 'official' Stoic line about grief, for instance, and advised moderation rather than eradication: 'when you've lost someone very close to you, to be endlessly stricken with grief is foolish self-indulgence, and to feel no grief is to be inhumanly insensitive.'[26]

Stoic warnings are traditionally meant to remind us that everything external is indifferent. But they could also help to counter the fear of death. For instance, Marcus recommends a 'trite but effective tactic' that involves remembering that all those who died old 'sleep six feet under', like everyone else. In the context of eternity all lives are brief, and a few extra years, even decades, count for nothing.[27]

If done in the right spirit these reminders could also help us to keep at the front of our mind the fact that time is short, so we had better allocate it on the basis of real priorities and appreciate what we have while we have it. As before, we should monitor the effect of these practices on us. If any distresses us, we should consider switching to a different one.

8. Consider the bigger picture

One of Marcus Aurelius' favourite methods is to place his life in perspective by imagining it within the context of space and time. He writes:

> 'To see them from above: the thousands of animal herds, the rituals, the voyages on calm or stormy seas, the different ways we come into the world, share it with one another, and leave it. Consider the lives led once by others, long ago, the lives to be led by others after you, the lives led even now, in foreign lands. How many people don't even know your name. How many will soon have forgotten it. How many offer you praise now – and tomorrow, perhaps, contempt.'[28]

A reliable way of achieving a sense of perspective and awe is by contemplating the night sky, or a photo taken through the Hubble Space Telescope. All around are mind-boggling numbers of galaxies just like ours, all containing inconceivably numerous stars like our sun and planets like our Earth. We don't know how far the universe stretches, where it is heading or what came before the Big Bang.

This kind of exercise could be disturbing as well as comforting. Focusing too much on the point of view of the universe might make all our pursuits appear trivial and meaningless. To be useful, that view should not supplant but supplement the human perspective that gives life meaning. It's better to shift between human and cosmic scale than get too caught up either in our little worlds or in the infinite cosmos.

We could also benefit from a more modest zooming out. Ask yourself: will this matter in an hour's time? Tomorrow? Next week? Next year? This can be effective in shrinking problems down, revealing their nature as nothing but temporary irritations.

9. Use common sense

Both Buddhism and Stoicism believed in making efforts to change ourselves rather than harbouring the delusion that changing our circumstances will bring us satisfaction. While we have to be aware of our limitations, this is generally the correct approach, since, as we have seen, we easily adapt to external changes and wind up no happier than before. The new car soon becomes simply the car that needs to be taken to the garage, the perfect new romance an all too typically complicated human relationship.

But that does not mean we are always wrong to think that a change is required to bring about an improvement. Imagine that, like Seneca, you are living above a bathhouse and are constantly assailed by a cacophony of noises: the grunts of the men doing weight training; people playing ball, singing or jumping 'into the swimming pool with a great splash'; 'the tweezer man screeching over and over in his shrill falsetto, just to attract attention: he is never silent unless he is plucking someone's armpits and making him cry out instead.'[29] Could we react as Seneca tried to do?

> 'I force my mind to pay attention to itself and not to be distracted by anything external. It does not matter what is making a noise outside, so long as there is no turmoil inside

– as long as there is no wrangling between desire and fear,
as long as greed is not at odds with self-indulgence, one
carping at the other. ... Only as the mind develops into
excellence do we achieve any real tranquillity.'

Probably not. Not even Seneca succeeded. He ends his story
on an unexpected note: '"What is it you're saying, then? Isn't
it easier sometimes to be away from the racket?" Yes, I grant
that, and that's why I'm going to leave this place.' We can often
get quite far by changing our attitude, but sometimes the right
thing to do is to tackle whatever external problem is bothering
us. There's no point in trying to achieve through spiritual practice what can be done by adopting simple practical measures.

10. Be quiet

On the question of speaking, Stoics and Buddhists are at one.
In Epictetus' words:

'Be mostly silent, or speak merely when necessary, and
in few words. We may enter sparingly into conversation
sometimes, when the occasion calls for it; but not about
any of the common subjects, such as gladiators, or horse
races, or athletic champions, or food, or drink – the vulgar
topics of conversation; and especially not about individuals, either to blame, or praise, or make comparisons.'[30]

The Buddha generally praised silence and consistently con-
demned pointless talk, which is said to consist of 'talk of kings,
robbers, ministers, armies, dangers, battles, food, drink, clothing, beds, garlands, perfumes, relatives, vehicles, villages,

towns, cities, countries, women, heroes, streets, wells, the dead, trifles, the origin of the world, the origin of the sea, whether things are so or are not so'.[31]

These are quite comprehensive lists. Does taking them seriously mean refraining from most conversation? If we don't follow the letter of the advice, what would it mean to apply its spirit? One discourse mentions three useful criteria for assessing speech: is it *truthful*? Is it *beneficial*? Is it *pleasing to others*? This is a good test that can be detached from the more austere command not to talk about anything trivial. It is not necessarily harmful to indulge in some daily gossip or chat about sport, and in fact such exchanges can be truthful and pleasing, even beneficial in the sense of oiling the wheels of social interaction and bringing some good humour to the day.

The texts recognise that of course these criteria can't always be fulfilled at once, so we are given some further advice: if something is not pleasing to others, the Buddha will still say it so long as it is truthful and beneficial.[32] We could use these questions to reflect on our usual patterns of conversation and decide for ourselves whether we need to revise the way we speak.

The traditions' praise of silence is also a useful corrective to our culture's emphasis on social networking, communication and extroversion. To be quiet today is to be considered almost pathological. Those of us who prefer to speak less and measure our words can feel encouraged by this.

Conclusion

As we have seen, both Buddhism and Stoicism in their different ways alert us to the unsatisfactoriness of existence. Things are transient, and lasting satisfaction is not for us to have. Impermanence, suffering and lack of control may or may not be ultimate truths of the universe, but they certainly capture our experience of the world when we attend carefully to it.

In the face of this situation, both traditions point to the necessity of accepting life warts and all, with all its impermanence and imperfection. In Buddhism, mindfulness meditation teaches us nothing if not acceptance of our actual experience, without clinging to it, denying it or pushing it away. In Stoicism there are regular exhortations to practise acceptance. Seneca, for instance, says: 'We have come into a world where life is lived on such terms: accept them and comply, or reject them and leave by whatever route you like.'[33]

None of this demands resignation; it just means that even when it's possible to make changes in our lives, acceptance is where we have to start from. What else could we do? Yet it's amazing how often we fight what actually is. We just can't accept that we made a mistake; that someone died; that a relationship ended.

Despite their insistence on acceptance, the traditions see themselves as offering a way out. But the sad fact is that imperfection can never be eradicated. Seeing clearly means giving up illusions of salvation and accepting life's unsatisfactoriness without antidotes. If it really were possible to end suffering by detaching ourselves from all things conventionally considered good, the price would be too high.

We can live fully in an imperfect world. This means embracing our contradictions: we are both rational and irrational, constrained but free. We have to honour the whole of who we are, body and mind, reason and emotion.

The common worldly goals that keep us in their grip – wealth, fame, success – have limited value for a good life. Even things that are genuinely valuable – life itself, health, relationships – are liable to fail us at any time. It would be wise therefore to rein in our desires and avoid making our well-being excessively dependent on their satisfaction.

We should remember 'how small ... the cup of human enjoyment is, how soon overflowed with tears',[34] therefore cherish precious impermanent things in the full knowledge that they will pass, like cherry blossom or autumn leaves. Their value is not diminished by their transience, and sadness is a fitting response to it.

We should cultivate clarity and curiosity, contentment and compassion. 'Life is short. That's all there is to say. Get what you can from the present – thoughtfully, justly', says Marcus.[35] We should not aim to make ourselves fortress-like, but to be vulnerable more wisely.

END NOTES

For full citations and copyright information, please refer to the References list, page 197.

Introduction

1. Seneca 2015, 64.9
2. *Kamma* and *nibbāna* in Pāli. Pāli is the language of much of the earliest Buddhist literature.
3. There are many lists in Buddhism – three refuges, five hindrances, five precepts, seven factors of awakening, ten perfections and so on, not to mention of course the four noble truths and the eight-fold path. Only a few of these have made it into my discussion, but for a 'list of Buddhist lists' see Leigh Brasington's website: leighb .com/listlist.htm. As for the scholarly debates currently ruffling feathers on many of the topics I touch on, clearly it would not have been possible to delve into them.

Chapter 1 – Setting the Scene

1. Snellgrove 2002, p. 7
2. '*Mahāpadāna Sutta*'. Walshe 1987, 14
3. E.g. Penner 2009; Gethin 1998, p. 16. But Stephen Batchelor points out that the little vignettes in the Pāli Canon describing daily life may well be truthful, since any later editors of the texts would have had no doctrinal reason to alter them.
4. Batchelor 2016
5. Diogenes Laertius, 9.61, 9.107
6. Beckwith 2015; Batchelor 2016

7. Diogenes Laertius, 9.62

8. James 1960, p. 69

9. '*Cūḷamāluṅkya Sutta*'. Gethin 2008, p. 171

10. '*Kevaddha Sutta*'. Walshe 1987, 11

11. Gethin 1998, p. 128. Anālayo (2016) also comments that as far as we can tell, the Buddha and his disciples believed in a variety of celestial beings (p. 59).

12. '*Sāmaññaphala Sutta*'. Gethin 2008, p. 31

13. Gethin 1998, p. 130

14. Diogenes Laertius, 7.147

15. Long 2002, pp. 145–6

16. Marcus Aurelius 2003, 6.36a

17. In Sellars 2006, pp. 91–2

18. Seneca 2015, 41.1

19. Sellars 2006, p. 93

20. Flanagan 2011, p. 3

Chapter 2 – *Dukkha* Happens: We Suffer

1. Giacomo Leopardi, 'Canto notturno di un pastore errante dell'Asia' (*Canti*, 23)

> *Vecchierel bianco, infermo,*
> *Mezzo vestito e scalzo,*
> *Con gravissimo fascio in su le spalle,*
> *Per montagna e per valle,*
> *Per sassi acuti, ed alta rena, e fratte,*
> *Al vento, alla tempesta, e quando avvampa*
> *L'ora, e quando poi gela,*
> *Corre via, corre, anela,*
> *Varca torrenti e stagni,*
> *Cade, risorge, e più e più s'affretta,*
> *Senza posa o ristoro,*
> *Lacero, sanguinoso; infin ch'arriva*

Colà dove la via
E dove il tanto affaticar fu volto:
Abisso orrido, immenso,
Ov'ei precipitando, il tutto obblia.
Vergine luna, tale
E' la vita mortale.

2. Nabokov, V. (2000) *Speak, Memory: An Autobiography Revisited*, Penguin, p. 5

3. Yalom 2008, pp. 9, 5

4. Diener and Biswas-Diener 2008, p. 157

5. Yalom 2008, p. 5

6. '*Jara Sutta*'. (SN 48.41), transl. Thanissaro Bhikkhu. *Access to Insight (BCBS Edition)*, 30 November 2013, http://www.accesstoinsight.org/tipitaka/sn/sn48/sn48.041.than.html

7. Fronsdal 2006, 11

8. Gombrich 2013, p. 10

9. '*Dhammacakkappavattana Sutta*' ('The Setting in Motion of the Wheel of the *Dhamma*'). Bodhi, 2005, p. 76. The Indian concept of *Dharma*, Pāli *Dhamma*, means the deep truth underlying everything, including moral truth. In Buddhism it also refers to the teaching of the Buddha.

10. '*Dhammacakkappavattana Sutta*'. Bodhi, 2005, p. 77

11. Bodhi 2005, p. 341

12. Gombrich 2013. This view is usually associated with the brahmanical tradition, to which the Buddha was supposed to be referring. According to Bronkhorst (2007), however, it is possible that both Buddhism and Brahmanism were in fact responding to ideas current at the time.

13. Collins 1994, pp. 66–75

14. Siderits 2007, p. 55

15. Sellars, 'Stoicism and the Human Condition', modernstoicism.com 10/12/2015

16. Marcus Aurelius 2003, 9.19

Chapter 3 – Maladies of the Soul: Why We Suffer

1. Sorabji 2000, p. 7. Sellars, 'Stoicism and Emotion', modernstoicism .com 1/2/2015

2. Depending on the thinker and the interpretation, emotions are seen as caused by or identical with beliefs. Inwood 1985, p. 131

3. 'Pleasure' and 'pain' might give the impression they are more physical than they are meant to be. Nussbaum 1994, p. 386

4. As reported by Cicero. Graver 2002, p. 43

5. Aristotle 2000, 2.6

6. Epictetus, 2.22

7. Long and Sedley 1987, p. 414

8. Graver 2002, pp. 59, 12, 60

9. In Nussbaum 1994, pp. 13–14

10. Musonius Rufus 2011, lecture 3

11. Graver 2002, p. 5

12. Seneca 2015, 8.2

13. Nussbaum 1994, p. 317

14. Nussbaum 1994, p. 15

15. Gethin 1998, p. 63

16. Bodhi 2005, p. 19

17. These distortions are known as *vipallāsas*.

18. '*Vipallāsa Sutta*'. (AN 4.49), transl. Andrew Olendzki. *Access to Insight (BCBS Edition)*, 2 November 2013. http://www.accesstoinsight.org/ tipitaka/an/an04/an04.049.olen.html

19. '*Alagaddūpama Sutta*'. Gethin 2008, p. 166

20. '*Salla Sutta*'. Bodhi 2005, p. 31. Anālayo 2013, p. 120

21. E.g. '*Sangīti Sutta*'. Walshe 1987, 33

22. Marcus Aurelius 2003, 8.28

23. Bodhi 2000, p. 1757

24. Bodhi 2005, p. 32

25. Although he was also aware of the limitations and dangers of relying solely on meditative experiences to gain knowledge (Anālayo 2003, p. 45).

26. Epictetus, 'Handbook 5'

Chapter 4 – How to Be Saved 1: Nirvana

1. Stephen Batchelor remarks that the 'Chapter of Eights', probably among the oldest strata of the Pāli Canon, shows no trace of many doctrines we now associate with Buddhism, including the four noble truths.

2. Bronkhorst (1993) suggests that the two views may reflect developments within Buddhism.

3. 'Cūḷamāluṅkya Sutta'. Gethin 2008, pp. 169. The question is dealt with indirectly and metaphorically, by saying that trying to answer is like speculating about the direction of a fire that has gone out ('Aggivacchagotta Sutta'. Ñāṇamoli and Bodhi 2009, 72).

4. Siderits 2007, p. 9

5. Anālayo 2015, p. 60

6. Anālayo 2003, p. 114

7. Griffiths 1981, p. 612

8. This is known as saññā-vedayita nirodha, or simply nirodha.

9. 'Mahāvedalla Sutta'. Ñāṇamoli and Bodhi 2009, 43. Griffiths 1981, p. 607

10. Bodhi 2012, p. 1323; Griffiths 1981, p. 608

11. Griffiths 1981. Keown (2001, pp. 65, 77) suggests that samatha was to cultivate moral virtue and vipassanā insight, since progress can be made through either.

12. Bronkhorst 1993

13. 'Pāsādika Sutta'. Walshe 1987, 29. Anālayo 2003, p. 79

14. Bodhi 2012, p. 946

15. In particular, that insight could be achieved with only a minimum of concentration and a focus on mindfulness (e.g., 'Mahāsatipaṭṭhāna Sutta', Walshe 1987, 22; Anālayo 2003, p. 84; Griffiths 1981, p. 615).

16. Anālayo 2003, p. 85; Bodhi 2012, pp. 535, 475, 1404

17. Anālayo 2003, pp. 85, 88–90. Gethin (2004) has also emphasised an integrated picture.

18. Gethin 2004. 'Saṅgārava Sutta'. Bodhi 2012, p. 807

19. James 1960, pp. 366–8

20. In the texts monks are sometimes said to suddenly attain awakening after hearing a particular teaching, but this event would normally have been preceded by lengthy training. Collins (1994) reminds us that nirvana is possible only for celibate monastics, as it involves eradication of desire (p. 61).

21. James 1960, p. 367

22. Immanuel Kant, 'Fundamental Principles of the Metaphysics of Moral'. In Wilson 2002, p. 168

23. According to d'Espagnat, mind-independent reality exists and generates knowledge, as there are links between such reality and ourselves. While science cannot give us actual descriptions of the things in themselves, it is conceivable that it could convey something of the nature of reality, although we can't be sure.

24. Nagel 1986, pp. 5–6

25. Johansson 1969, p. 102. '*Sappurisa Sutta*'. Ñāṇamoli and Bodhi 2009, 113

26. Gethin 1998, p. 77

27. Bodhi 2000, p. 1294

28. Anālayo 2015, p. 11; 2016, pp. 15–16, 73

29. The Buddha argues against nirvana as conventional health and well-being in the '*Māgandiya Sutta*'. Ñāṇamoli and Bodhi 2009, 75. Anālayo 2003, p. 257

30. Bhante Bodhidhamma, personal communication

Chapter 5 – How to Be Saved 2: Living in Accordance with Nature

1. Many authors point out that *eudaimonia* does not really mean happiness, only to go on to follow convention and use 'happiness' as a translation, as if all we need to do is issue the warning. I find that the more established meaning keeps reasserting itself, so it is difficult to read 'happiness' as anything other than a state of mind. In these cases I always feel I'm constantly having to perform an instantaneous mental translation.

2. 'Virtue' is also a slightly misleading translation, as it refers generally to the qualities that are distinctive of human beings and not only to moral qualities, but I find 'excellence' even more misleading, as many of the qualities were indeed moral qualities.

3. Other items in the world also partake of this organising principle, called *pneuma*, but they are 'tuned' at different tensions.

4. Musonius Rufus 2011, lecture 17

5. Seneca 2014, 'Consolation to Helvia', p. 53

6. The main virtues in Greek philosophy were traditionally justice, wisdom, temperance and courage, but these were widely thought of as unified.

7. Seneca 2015, 73.16

8. Diogenes Laertius, 7.89. Inwood 1985, p. 68

9. Graver 2002, pp. 3, 4

10. Epictetus, 1.22

11. Epictetus, 3.3

12. Diogenes Laertius, 7.102

13. Epictetus, 4.1

14. Epictetus, 4.7

15. We should remember that, in the world of the Stoics, people's station in life was a lot more fixed, without the social mobility and career and travel options we have today, not to mention the constant message that we can be whoever we want to be.

16. Epictetus, 4.10

17. Epictetus, 4.1

18. Epictetus, 'Handbook 17', 4.1

19. If emotions can be divided into pleasure, pain, desire and fear, it is only for the latter two that the halfway house of selections and deselections is provided. With pleasure and pain we need to train ourselves to achieve genuine indifference.

20. Wilson 2015, p. 12

21. Reinhold Niebuhr (lived 1892–1971)

22. Diogenes Laertius, 7.37

23. Sorabji 2000, pp. 8, 169, 173

24. Nussbaum 1994, p. 41

25. Nussbaum 2001, p. 232; also pp. 23, 106, 109, 115, 117, 125, 200. Emotions are not necessarily associated with particular bodily feelings, but they seem different from other kinds of judgements because 'the experience of emotion usually ... contains rich and dense perceptions of the object, which are highly concrete and replete with detail' (p. 65). They are also different from bodily appetites (more specific and automatic), moods (more vague) and desires (more linked to motivation) (pp. 24, 130–1).

26. Nussbaum 2001, p. 42

27. Nussbaum 1994, p. 370

28. Nussbaum 2001, p. 22

29. Marcus Aurelius 2003, 8.48

30. Nussbaum 1994, p. 235

31. Graver 2002, p. 7

32. Graver 2002, pp. 7, 8, 13

33. Nussbaum 2016, pp. 95, 140

34. Nussbaum 1994, p. 501

35. Dryden 2002, pp. 48–51. We are often reminded that Albert Ellis was originally inspired by Stoicism, and among modern psychotherapies REBT does indeed come closest to the Stoics' challenging stance. But in relation to the emotions the ethos of REBT is in fact more of an Aristotelian one.

36. Damasio 2000

Chapter 6 – More Than Happiness

1. Taylor 2007

2. It is also actually harder than one might think, as metaphysical assumptions have a way of creeping in, and before we know it we might be, for instance, disavowing our emotions in unhelpful ways.

3. Kurzban 2010, p. 142

4. Gaia House retreat 2017

5. There are different terms in Pāli that can be translated as happiness, pleasure, joy, bliss or rapture, and the translations are not always consistent with each other.

6. Seneca 2015, 59.15

7. Seneca 2015, 59.2

8. Seneca 2015, 59.2

9. Seneca 2015, 98.1

10. Seneca 2014, 'On the Happy Life', p. 243

11. Seneca 2015, 59.17

12. Norman 1985, p. 127

13. Dalai Lama and Cutler 1998, p. 3

14. Fronsdal 2006, 1

15. *'Mahāsaccaka Sutta'*. Ñāṇamoli and Bodhi 2009, 36

16. *'Mahāgosinga Sutta'*. Ñāṇamoli and Bodhi 2009, 32. Anālayo 2003, p. 165

17. *'Mahādukkhakkhanda Sutta'*. Ñāṇamoli and Bodhi 2009, 13.

18. *'Potaliya Sutta'*. Ñāṇamoli and Bodhi 2009, 54

19. *'Laṭukikopama Sutta'*. Ñāṇamoli and Bodhi 2009, 66

20. *'Kandaraka Sutta'*. Ñāṇamoli and Bodhi 2009, 51. Anālayo 2003, p. 167

21. *'Poṭṭhapāda Sutta'*. Walshe 1987, 9

22. *'Bālapaṇḍita Sutta'*. Ñāṇamoli and Bodhi 2009, 129

23. *'Saḷāyatanavibhanga Sutta'*. Ñāṇamoli and Bodhi 2009, 137. Anālayo 2003, p. 166; Anālayo 2013, p. 132. In the same discourse, the Buddha makes a distinction between six kinds of joy based on the household life (which arise from agreeable or gratifying forms, sounds, odours, flavours and mind-objects) and six kinds of joy based on renunciation (knowing the impermanence of all the above).

24. Anālayo 2013, pp. 100–1

25. Kobayashi Issa, http://poetsonline.blogspot.co.uk/2013/04/cherry-blossom-haiku-and-seasons.html

26. *'Subha Sutta'*. Ñāṇamoli and Bodhi 2009, 99. Anālayo 2003, p. 166. *'Brahmajāla Sutta'*. Walshe 1987, 1. Anālayo 2013, pp. 77–9.

27. 'Sāmaññaphala Sutta'. Gethin 2008, pp. 28–9
28. Marcus Aurelius 2003, 5.1
29. Seneca 2014, 'On the Happy Life', p. 247
30. 'Mahāparinibbāṇa Sutta'. Walshe 1987, 16
31. Keown 2001, pp. 38–9, 76
32. Traditionally the two formulations are linked as follows: right view and intention are said to come under wisdom; right speech, action and livelihood under morality; and right effort, mindfulness and concentration under meditation/concentration ('Cūḷavedalla Sutta'. Ñāṇamoli and Bodhi 2009, 44). But, arguably, all the elements of the eightfold path are in some way connected with ethics.
33. Rahula 1967, p. 46
34. 'Soṇadaṇḍa Sutta'. Walshe 1987, 4. Harvey 2000, p. 11; Keown 2001, pp. 38–9
35. Seneca 2015, 95.57
36. Keown 2001, pp. 111–12; Gethin 1998, pp. 83–4
37. While it is used mostly in relation to concentration practices (*samatha*) and the *jhānas*, sometimes it refers to insight practices (*vipassanā*), or walking meditation (Anālayo 1993, pp. 72–3).
38. Rahula 1967, p. 46
39. This occurs in another threefold formula: *dāna, sīla, bhāvanā* (*dāna* meaning generosity and *sīla* ethical conduct, as before).
40. Gethin 1998, p. 174
41. Rahula 1967, p. 74
42. Gombrich 2013, p. 172

Chapter 7 – Removing the Dust from Our Eyes

1. 'Ariyapariyesanā Sutta'. Ñāṇamoli and Bodhi 2009, 26
2. 'Chapter of Eights', *Sutta Nipāta*, 787, transl. Stephen Batchelor, unpublished
3. According to Gombrich (1996), the Buddha may initially have had limited interest in putting forward a coherent philosophy, but this may have developed through preaching and dialogue (p. 31).

4. *'Brahmajāla Sutta'*. Walshe 1987, 1. Some of these do seem to represent the Buddha's own views, but still they are not things it is useful to talk about (Gombrich 2013, p. 166).

5. *'Alagaddūpama Sutta'*. Ñāṇamoli and Bodhi 2009, 22

6. Hadot 1995, p. 60

7. Bodhi 2012, p. 74

8. *'Mahāsaccaka Sutta'*. Ñāṇamoli and Bodhi 2009, 36. Bronkhorst (1993), however, points out that elsewhere the Buddha is reported as approving of some of these.

9. Diogenes Laertius, 6

10. Epictetus, 4.1. Seneca 2015, 92

11. Epictetus, 4.11

12. But the Stoics are not dualist in a typical sense, and the mind is considered a 'physical' object.

13. Epictetus, 'Handbook 33'

14. Musonius Rufus 2011, lecture 20

15. Musonius Rufus 2011, lectures 19, 21, 20

16. Seneca 2015, 123.13

17. Musonius Rufus 2011, fragment 34

18. Seneca 2014, 'On the Happy Life', p. 242

19. Seneca 2014, 'On the Happy Life', pp. 259, 258

20. Seneca 2015, 74.18

21. Seneca 2014, 'On the Happy Life', p. 255

22. Seneca 2015, 119.9

23. While Seneca's work supposedly draws on his own life, it should not be considered straightforwardly autobiographical, as much of it follows established literary genres and has social and political goals as subtext.

24. Bodhi 2005, pp. 32–3

25. Fronsdal 2006, 5

26. Kenrick and Griskevicius 2013, p. 30

27. Wright (2017) strongly expresses the view that the Buddhist path, and in particular the experience of not-self, represents a rebellion against the values of natural selection.

28. Abraham Maslow, twentieth-century American psychologist.
29. Westacott 2016, pp. 94–6, 205
30. Aristotle 2000, 1.5
31. Aristotle 2000, 10.8; 1.10
32. Aristotle 2000, 8.1
33. Reason was divided into theoretical (*sophia*), which was about contemplating unchangeable truths, and practical (*phronēsis*), which instead was about making choices in the world.
34. Aristotle 2000, 10.8
35. Even if determining exactly what that means can be daunting.
36. Aristotle 2000, 3.9
37. Gaskin 1995, p. 49
38. May 2017
39. Gaskin 1995, p. 6
40. Dittmar 2014
41. Kurzban 2010, p. 4
42. Kurzban 2010, p. 24
43. Kurzban 2010, p. 44
44. Kurzban 2010
45. The cognitive processes responsible for these are e.g. selective memory and faulty inferences. Kahneman 2011; Kurzban 2010.
46. Philosopher Daniel Dennett has described the self as a 'centre of narrative gravity'. Dennett 1993.
47. Not everyone would agree that there is a necessary connection between not-self and the arising of compassion.
48. But some kind of non-physical consciousness is also entertained in Buddhism, and we have no reason to believe in *that*.
49. It's worth reminding ourselves that what the Buddha denied was not this 'daily' self but the notion of an unchanging core, more like a soul, which was upheld by other Indian traditions. 'The not-self teaching is only about the absence of an unchanging, permanent self. But the five aggregates as a process certainly exist' (Anālayo 2013, p. 91).
50. Inwood 1985, p. 138

51. John Sellars, personal communication
52. Harris 2015, p. 43
53. Marcus Aurelius 2003, 5.10

Chapter 8 – The Sage and the Buddha: Models for Living

1. '*Ariyapariyesanā Sutta*'. Ñāṇamoli and Bodhi 2009, 26
2. Fronsdal 2006, 14
3. Musonius Rufus 2011, lecture 2
4. Epictetus, 4.1. Although this does sometimes produce strange perspectives: '"Come now, Epictetus, take off your beard." – If I am a philosopher, I answer, I will not take it off. – "Then I will take off your head." – If that will do you any good, take it off' (1.2).
5. '*Bāhitika Sutta*'. Ñāṇamoli and Bodhi 2009, 88
6. '*Pāsādika Sutta*'. Walshe 1987, 29
7. '*Samaṇamaṇḍikā Sutta*'. Ñāṇamoli and Bodhi 2009, 78. Anālayo 2003, p. 258
8. Sellars 2006, p. 37; 2009, p. 60
9. Brennan 2003, p. 271
10. Inwood 1985, p. 182; Sellars 2009, p. 60
11. In Sellars 2006, p. 38; 2009, p. 63
12. Epictetus, 'Handbook 51'; 4.12
13. This begins with things like visiting and paying respect to a teacher, memorising the teaching, and so on. '*Kīṭāgiri Sutta*'. Ñāṇamoli and Bodhi 2009, 70
14. Becker 1998, p. 82
15. '*Cūḷahatthipadopama Sutta*'. Ñāṇamoli and Bodhi 2009, 27
16. Gethin 1998, p. 173
17. Seneca 2015, 94
18. Seneca 2015, 94
19. '*Bāhitika Sutta*'. Ñāṇamoli and Bodhi 2009, 88
20. '*Kālāma Sutta*'. Bodhi 2012, p. 280
21. The Stoics consider it impossible to judge that an action is appropriate (*kathēkon*) and feel motivated to do something else.

22. Seneca 2015, 95

23. Bhante Bodhidhamma, personal communication

24. Anālayo 2015, pp. 30–1. *'Sāmagāma Sutta'*. Ñāṇamoli and Bodhi 2009, 104

25. *'Cūḷagosiṅga Sutta'*. Ñāṇamoli and Bodhi 2009, 31

26. Anālayo 2015, pp. 32–5

27. Anālayo 2015, pp. 36–7

28. Bodhi 2012, p. 1066

29. Seneca 2010, 'On Anger', p. 60

30. Anālayo 2015, p. 38. Bodhi 2000, p. 1609

31. Anālayo 2015, p. 41. *'Mahārāhulovāda Sutta'*. Ñāṇamoli and Bodhi 2009, 62

32. Cultivating the immeasurables has many benefits, but it is said that to attain liberation other parts of the path are also necessary. *'Mahāgovinda Sutta'*. Walshe 1987, 19

33. Epictetus, 2.10. Nussbaum 1994, pp. 342–4; Sellars 2006, p. 131

34. Seneca 2015, 95.52

35. Epictetus, 2.22. Sorabji 2000, p. 184

36. Epictetus, 3.3

37. Nussbaum 1994, p. 496; 2001, p. 356

38. Long 2002, p. 253

39. Anālayo 2015, p. 13. There are two, interrelated, words in Pāli that are translated as compassion: *anukampa* arises naturally and is often used in relation to the Buddha's own motivations. *Karuṇā* is more of a technical concept, and refers mainly to a state to be cultivated in meditation.

40. Anālayo 2015, p. 5

41. Aronson 1980, p. 65

42. Anālayo 2015, p. 6

43. Anālayo 2015, p. 47

44. Anālayo 2015

45. Bloom 2017, p. 41

46. Translating this into Buddhist terms, we could call the resource-seeking system, greed; the threat system, aversion; and the soothing and affiliation system, kindness and compassion.

47. Gilbert 2013

48. Gilbert 2013, p. 294. C. Germer, *The Mindful Path to Self-Compassion*, as cited in Gilbert 2013, p. 270

49. Striker 1996, p. 186

50. Anālayo 2015, p. 41

51. Anālayo 2015, pp. 48, 45

52. Bhante Bodhidhamma, personal communication

53. Aronson 1980, p. 90

54. '*Sakkapañhā Sutta*'. Walshe 1987, 21. Anālayo 2015, p. 43

55. Nussbaum 1994, p. 363. This sentence, reported by Cicero, is said to have been uttered by the philosopher Anaxagoras.

56. '*Khaggavisāṇa Sutta: A Rhinoceros*' (Sn 1.3), transl. Thanissaro Bhikkhu. *Access to Insight (BCBS Edition)*, 30 November 2013, http://www.accesstoinsight.org/tipitaka/kn/snp/snp.1.03.than.html

57. Sellars, 'Hard Truths and Happiness', modernstoicism.com 3/12/2016. Epictetus, 'Handbook 3'

58. '*Ariyapariyesanā Sutta*'. Ñāṇamoli and Bodhi 2009, 26

59. Epictetus, 2.22

60. '*Sallekha Sutta*'. Ñāṇamoli and Bodhi 2009, 8. Anālayo 2015, p. 17

61. May 2017, p. 197

62. Yalom 2008, p. 109

63. May 2017, p. viii

Chapter 9 – Spiritual Practice: Beyond Theory

1. Anālayo 2013, p. 237

2. Epictetus, 3.21

3. Epictetus, 3.21

4. Seneca 2015, 71.31

5. This is part of the Buddhist theory of 'dependent arising', which is complex and controversial and usually taken to apply over three lifetimes, but this particular section must be easily recognisable in everybody's experience.

6. Anālayo, 'Mindfulness in Early Buddhist Meditation' (course material from 2016 Sharpham House retreat), p. 32
7. This mental proliferation is called *papañca*.
8. This is determined by the nature of the impression and the state of the agent who receives it.
9. Sellars 2006, p. 65. Epictetus, fragment 9
10. Seneca 2010, 'On Anger' p. 36
11. Epictetus, 1.1
12. Kahneman 2011, p. 90. Kurzban (2010) writes that the relevant modules are likely to be many more than two. But Kahneman (2011) himself explains that we need to take these 'fictitious characters' with a pinch of salt (p. 29).
13. Kahneman 2011, pp. 24, 44
14. Wilson (2002) suggests that we can learn more about ourselves by looking at our own behaviour, or how other people see us, than by introspection.
15. Control of attention is shared by both System 1 and System 2 (Kahneman 2011, p. 22).
16. Hadot 1995, p. 59
17. Seneca 2015, 94.72
18. Seneca 2015, 4.7
19. Marcus Aurelius 2003, 9.32
20. Musonius Rufus 2011, lecture 6
21. Epictetus, 2.18
22. '*Dvedhāvitakka Sutta*'. Ñāṇamoli and Bodhi 2009, 19
23. Marcus Aurelius 2003, 5.16
24. Bentham, J. (1789) *An Introduction to the Principles of Morals and Legislation*, ch. 1
25. Gethin 2015. Anālayo 2003, p. 47; 2013, pp. 30–2
26. According to a later distinction in Buddhism, attention is a basic function that is just there all the time, while mindfulness has to be developed.
27. '*Dvedhāvitakka Sutta*'. Ñāṇamoli and Bodhi 2009, 19
28. Gethin 2015, p. 31

29. Claxton 2016, p. 66
30. Anālayo 2003, p. 60
31. Anālayo 2003, pp. 50, 52. 'Mahācattārīsaka Sutta'. Ñāṇamoli and Bodhi 2009, 117
32. 'Mahā-Assapura Sutta'. Ñāṇamoli and Bodhi 2009, 39. Anālayo 2003, pp. 60, 55; 2013, pp. 28–30
33. 'Cātumā Sutta'. Ñāṇamoli and Bodhi 2009, 67. Anālayo 2003, p. 57
34. Epictetus, 'Handbook 48'
35. Epictetus, 4.12
36. Seneca 2010, 'On Anger', p. 21
37. Epictetus, 'Handbook 34'
38. 'Vitakkasaṇṭhāna Sutta'. (MN 20) transl. Soma Thera. Access to Insight (BCBS Edition), 10 January 2013, http://www.accesstoinsight.org/tipitaka/mn/mn.020.soma.html
39. E.g., Harris 2009. ACT was developed by Steve Hayes.
40. Bernstein et al. 2015
41. May, R. (1975) The Courage to Create, W. W. Norton, ch. 5
42. Gethin 2015, p. 14
43. Marcus Aurelius 2003, 12.18
44. Marcus Aurelius 2003, 6.13, 2.2, 4.48
45. Anālayo 2013, p. 63
46. Anālayo 2003, p. 153
47. Bodhi 2000, p. 1773. Anālayo 2003, p. 149
48. Montaigne, 'On Physiognomy', p. 1189
49. Seneca 2015, 99.9, 26.7
50. Anālayo 2016, p. 207

Chapter 10 – Meditations for a Better Life

1. Seneca 2010, 'On Anger', p. 71
2. Epictetus, 4.6
3. Bodhi 2000, p. 1529
4. Seneca 2010, 'On Anger', p. 66
5. Epictetus, 'Handbook 5'

6. Epictetus, 'Handbook 3'
7. Seneca 2015, 8.5
8. Marcus Aurelius 2003, 7.67
9. Seneca, 'Letter 7'. https://en.wikisource.org/wiki/Moral_letters_to_Lucilius/Letter_7
10. Epictetus, 'Handbook 33'
11. Anālayo 2003, p. 161. '*Brahmajāla Sutta*'. Walshe 1987, 1
12. Seneca 2014, 'On the Shortness of Life', p. 132
13. Marcus Aurelius 2003, 2.1
14. Seneca 2010, 'On Anger', p. 41
15. Epictetus, 'Handbook 42'
16. Marcus Aurelius 2003, 7.22
17. Anālayo 2015, pp. 23–4
18. Epictetus, 2.5
19. Seneca 2015, 96.3
20. Seneca 2015, 91.8
21. Seneca 2015, 107.3
22. Seneca 2015, 13
23. The fifth truth is: 'I am the owner of my karma; I am born of my karma; I live supported by my karma; I will inherit my karma; whatever I do, whether good or evil, that I will inherit.'
24. Anālayo 2016, p. 121
25. Epictetus, 3.24
26. Seneca 2014, 'Consolation to Helvia', p. 66
27. Marcus Aurelius 2003, 4.50
28. Marcus Aurelius 2003, 9.30
29. Seneca 2015, 56.15
30. Epictetus, 'Handbook 33'
31. '*Sandaka Sutta*', Ñāṇamoli and Bodhi 2009, 76
32. '*Abhayarājakumāra Sutta*', Ñāṇamoli and Bodhi 2009, 58. Anālayo 2015, p. 9
33. Seneca 2015, 91.15
34. Okakura 2016, p. 4
35. Marcus Aurelius 2003, 4.26

REFERENCES

Buddhism

Anālayo (2016) *Mindfully Facing Disease and Death*. Windhorse Publications. © 2016 by Bhikkhu Anālayo, quotations reproduced here by arrangement with Windhorse Publications.

Anālayo (2015) *Compassion and Emptiness in Early Buddhist Meditation*. Windhorse Publications. © 2015 by Bhikkhu Anālayo, quotations reproduced here by arrangement with Windhorse Publications.

Anālayo (2013) *Perspectives on Satipaṭṭhāna*. Windhorse Publications. © 2013 by Bhikkhu Anālayo, quotations reproduced here by arrangement with Windhorse Publications.

Anālayo (2003) *Satipaṭṭhāna: The Direct Path to Realization*. Windhorse Publications. © 2003 by Bhikkhu Anālayo, quotations reproduced here by arrangement with Windhorse Publications.

Aronson, H. B. (1980) *Love and Sympathy in Theravāda Buddhism*. Motilal Banarsidass

Batchelor, S. (2016) Greek Buddha: Pyrrho's Encounter with Early Buddhism in Central Asia. *Contemporary Buddhism*, 17, 1

Bodhi, Bhikkhu (2012) *The Numerical Discourses of the Buddha: A Translation of the Anguttara Nikāya*. Wisdom Publications. © 2012 Bhikkhu Bodhi, quotations reproduced here by arrangement with Wisdom Publications, Inc., wisdompubs.org.

Bodhi, Bhikkhu (2005) *In the Buddha's Words: An Anthology of Discourses from the Pāli Canon*. Wisdom Publications. © 2005 Bhikkhu Bodhi, quotations reproduced here by arrangement with Wisdom Publications, Inc., wisdompubs.org.

Bodhi, Bhikkhu (2000) *The Connected Discourses of the Buddha*. Wisdom Publications. © 2000 Bhikkhu Bodhi, quotations reproduced here by arrangement with Wisdom Publications, Inc., wisdompubs.org.

Bronkhorst, J. (2007) *Greater Magadha*. Brill

Bronkhorst, J. (1993) *The Two Traditions of Meditation in Ancient India*. Motilal Banarsidass

Collins, S. (1994) What are Buddhists *doing* when they deny the self? In F. E. Reynolds and D. Tracy, *Religion and Practical Reason*. State University of New York Press

Dalai Lama, H.H. and Cutler, H. (1998) *The Art of Happiness*. Hodder and Stoughton

Flanagan, O. (2011) *The Bodhisattva's Brain*. MIT Press

Fronsdal, G. (2006) *The Dhammapada*. Shambhala Publications

Gethin, R. (2015) Buddhist conceptualisations of mindfulness. In K. W. Brown, J. D. Creswell and R. M. Ryan, *Handbook of Mindfulness*. The Guilford Press

Gethin, R. (2008) *Sayings of the Buddha*. Oxford University Press. Extracts reproduced here by permission of Oxford University Press.

Gethin, R. (2004) On the practice of Buddhist meditation. *Buddhismus in Geschichte und Gegenwart* 9

Gethin, R. (1998) *The Foundations of Buddhism*. Oxford University Press

Gombrich, R. F. (2013) *What the Buddha Thought*. Equinox

Gombrich, R. F. (1996) *How Buddhism Began*. Munshiram Manoharlal

Griffiths, P. (1981) Concentration or insight. *Journal of the American Academy of Religion*, 49, 4

Harvey, P. (2000) *An Introduction to Buddhist Ethics*. Cambridge University Press

Johansson, R. E. A. (1969) *The Psychology of Nirvana*. Allen and Unwin

Keown, D. (2001) *The Nature of Buddhist Ethics*. Palgrave

Ñāṇamoli, Bhikkhu and Bodhi, Bhikkhu (2009) *The Middle Length Discourses of the Buddha: A Translation of the Majjhima Nikāya*. Wisdom Publications. © 1995 Bhikkhu Bodhi, quotations reproduced here by arrangement with Wisdom Publications, Inc., wisdompubs.org.

Norman, K. R. (1985) *The Rhinoceros Horn*. Pali Text Society

Penner, H. H. (2009) *Rediscovering the Buddha*. Oxford University Press

Rahula, W. (1967) *What the Buddha Taught*. Gordon Fraser

Siderits, M. (2007) *Buddhism as Philosophy*. Ashgate

Snellgrove, D. (2002) *Indo-Tibetan Buddhism*. Shambhala Publications

Walshe, M. (1987) *The Long Discourses of the Buddha: A Translation of the Dīgha Nikāya*. Wisdom Publications.
© Maurice Walshe, 1987, 1995, 2012, quotations reproduced here by arrangement with Wisdom Publications, Inc., wisdompubs.org.

Wright, R. (2017) *Why Buddhism Is True*. Simon & Schuster

Stoicism

Becker, L. C. (1998) *A New Stoicism*. Princeton University Press

Brennan, T. (2003) Stoic Moral Psychology. In B. Inwood, *The Cambridge Companion to the Stoics*. Cambridge University Press

Graver, M. (2002) *Cicero on the Emotions*. The University of Chicago Press. © 2002 by The University of Chicago, quotations reproduced here by arrangement with The University of Chicago Press.

Epictetus, *The Discourses, The Handbook, Fragments* (transl. T. Wentworth Higginson). Accessed at http://files.libertyfund.org/pll/titles/1477.html (original publisher Little, Brown, and Co. 1865). Edited by the author.

Hadot, P. (1995) *Philosophy as a Way of Life*. Blackwell

Inwood, B. (1985) *Ethics and Human Action in Early Stoicism*. Oxford University Press

Long, A. A. (2002) *Epictetus*. Oxford University Press

Long, A. A. and Sedley, D. N. (1987) *The Hellenistic Philosophers*. Cambridge University Press

Marcus Aurelius (2003) *Meditations* (transl. G. Hays). Weidenfeld and Nicolson. Translation copyright © 2002 by Penguin Random House LLC. Used by permission of Modern Library, an imprint of Random House, a division of Penguin Random House LLC. All rights reserved.

Musonius Rufus (2011) *Lectures & Sayings* (transl. C. King). CreateSpace

Nussbaum, M. C. (2016) *Anger and Forgiveness*. Oxford University Press

Nussbaum, M. C. (2001) *Upheavals of Thought*. Cambridge University Press

Nussbaum, M. C. (1994) *The Therapy of Desire*. Princeton University Press

Sellars, J. (2009) *The Art of Living*. Duckworth

Sellars, J. (2006) *Stoicism*. Acumen

Seneca (2015) *Letters on Ethics* (transl. M. Graver and A. A. Long). The University of Chicago Press. Quotations © 2015 by The University of Chicago, reproduced here by arrangement with The University of Chicago Press.

Seneca (2014) *Hardship and Happiness* (transl. E. Fantham, H. M. Nine, J. Ker and G. D. Williams). The University of Chicago Press. © 2014 by The University of Chicago, quotations reproduced here by arrangement with The University of Chicago Press.

Seneca (2010) *Anger, Mercy, Revenge* (transl. R. A. Master and M. C. Nussbaum). The University of Chicago Press. © 2014 by The University of Chicago, quotations reproduced here by arrangement with The University of Chicago Press.

Sorabji, R. (2000) *Emotion and Peace of Mind*. Oxford University Press

Striker, G. (1996) *Essays on Hellenistic Epistemology and Ethics*. Cambridge University Press

Wilson, E. (2015) *Seneca: A Life*. Allen Lane

General

Aristotle (2000) *Nicomachean Ethics* (ed. R. Crisp). Cambridge University Press

Beckwith, C. I. (2015) *Greek Buddha*. Princeton University Press

Bernstein, A. et al. (2015) Decentering and related constructs: a critical review and metacognitive processes model. *Perspectives on Psychological Science*, 10, 5

Bloom, P. (2017) *Against Empathy*. Bodley Head

Claxton, G. (2016) How conscious experience comes about, and why meditation is helpful. In M. A. West, *The Psychology of Meditation*. Oxford University Press

Damasio, A. (2000) *The Feeling of What Happens*. Vintage

Dennett, D. (1993) *Consciousness Explained*. Penguin

Diener, E. and Biswas-Diener, R. (2008) *Happiness: Unlocking the mysteries of psychological wealth*. Blackwell

Diogenes Laertius, *Lives of the Eminent Philosophers* (ed. R. D. Hicks). Accessed at http://data.perseus.org/citations/urn:cts:greekLit:tlg0004.tlg001.perseus-eng1:1 (original publisher Harvard University Press 1972, first published 1925)

Dittmar, H. et al. (2014) The relationship between materialism and personal well-being: a meta-analysis. *Journal of Personality and Social Psychology*, 107, 5

Dryden, W. (2002) *Fundamentals of Rational Emotive Behaviour Therapy*. Whurr

d'Espagnat, B. (1983) *In Search of Reality*. Springer-Verlag

Gaskin, J. (1995) *The Epicurean Philosophers*. J. M. Dent

Gilbert, P. and Choden (2013) *Mindful Compassion*. Robinson

Harris, R. (2009) *ACT Made Simple*. New Harbinger Publications

Harris, S. (2015) *Waking Up*. Black Swan

James, W. (1960) *The Varieties of Religious Experience*. Fount

Kahneman, D. (2011) *Thinking, Fast and Slow*. Allen Lane

Kenrick, D. T. and Griskevicius, V. (2013) *The Rational Animal*. Basic Books

Kurzban, R. (2010) *Why Everyone (Else) is a Hypocrite*. Princeton University Press

May, T. (2017) *A Fragile Life*. University of Chicago Press

Montaigne, M. de (1987). *The Complete Essays*. Penguin

Nagel, T. (1986) *The View from Nowhere*. Oxford University Press

O'Keefe (2010) *Epicureanism*. Acumen

Okakura, Kakuzo (2016) *The Book of Tea*. Penguin

Taylor, C. (2007) *A Secular Age*. Belknap Harvard

Westacott, E. (2016) *The Wisdom of Frugality*. Princeton University Press

Wilson, T. D. (2002) *Strangers to Ourselves*. Belknap Harvard

Yalom, I. D. (2008) *Staring at the Sun*. Piatkus

ACKNOWLEDGEMENTS

I would like to thank all those who have generously spared me some time to talk about issues related to this book, on this and/or previous occasions. They are: Bhante Anālayo, Stephen Batchelor, Bhante Bodhidhamma, Rupert Gethin, Richard Gombrich, Keith Seddon, John Sellars, and Richard Sorabji. A special thank you to Dan Clurman, who helped me to think clearly, all those years ago. Thank you to Stephen Batchelor and Tim LeBon for reading and commenting on an earlier version of this book, to my editor Kiera Jamison for helping to make this book a lot clearer, and to Duncan Heath and everyone at Icon Books. The greatest thanks to Julian Baggini. Needless to say, any errors are my own.

INDEX